Develop Your Soft Skills

for Success as a Consultant

Don Wynn

The Brass Tree

Satellite Beach, Florida

THE BRASS TREE

ISBN: 978-0-615-67675-3

To my wife
Dixie

Table of Contents

Preface

If you are reading this book, you must be a consultant of some sort or you must be thinking about becoming a consultant. In either case, this book should serve you well. I have worked as a consultant on a full time basis for over 20 years and this book represents some of the little tips that I have learned over that time. I have had mentors who shared their knowledge with me and I have been an avid observer of people and especially of how they interact. My own mistakes have provided me with experiences that I don't want to repeat. This book is an attempt to pass on the things that I have learned from all of these sources.

To be successful as a consultant; you must have specific business or technical skills that are important to clients and prospective clients. Clients must be willing to pay for your services. Having those business and technical skills alone is not enough to guarantee your success. If solid knowledge and skills is not enough, then what else do you need?

Simply put, you need to understand how to interact with clients, you need to know how to present yourself and you need to understand the nuances of a consulting career. This book is about simple little things that can have a dramatic impact on your success. You might say 'well that's just common sense.' And that would certainly be true but most of us don't apply common sense approaches to our lives or to our work unless we make a conscious attempt to do so.

Many of these little gems were learned as the result of mistakes that I have made, some more than once. Some people may naturally have good interpersonal skills but everyone can improve if they will just give some thought to it.

Without that conscious effort to eliminate these little mistakes, you are likely to repeat them on some routine basis. If you do taht, you will be setting a pattern that people around you will notice.

I refer to consulting and to technology consulting in this book many times because that is the career area I have chosen and where I have worked for a major portion of my life. The little tips were learned during my career as a consultant but they apply to almost any occupation where you have to interact with people. The key to any lesson is to find a way to apply it to your specific situation. That is my challenge to you.

If you apply some of the ideas that you learn in this book, you will become a better consultant regardless of the specific business area where you work. It will help you enhance your relationship with your clients and with their employees. Your career will be more fulfilling and you will gain a greater sense of satisfaction.

Having outstanding skills in the business area where you work is not enough. Those skills are the meat and potatoes of your tool set. You have to present yourself well as you perform your consulting duties.

You Can't be an Eagle if You Don't Jump

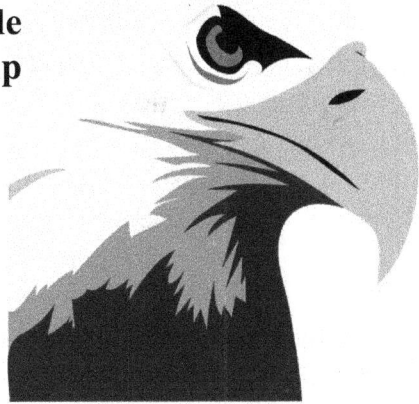

A small bird sat perched on the side of the nest looking down at what seemed to be a terrifying height. This little bird had reached a time in his life when he had to make a very important decision. The young bird hesitated at the edge and then moved quickly back to the safety of the nest. His mother circled patiently above. After some time, the little bird approached the edge of the nest again. This renewed spirit got him to the edge of the nest but, once again, the little bird quickly moved back from the edge.

After several such attempts, the mother bird landed in the nest and nudged him toward the edge. The mother bird uttered an encouraging cry and took flight. The little bird then spread his tiny wings and stepped off into nothing. At first, he faltered but the wind caught his wings and he realized the joy of flight. With his mother by his side, he soared above the treetops.

The message here is that you can't be an eagle if you don't jump!

Fear of the unknown, the untried or the untraveled road is a normal, human emotion. However, fear is usually followed by a period of indecision. If you want to be great at what you do, you cannot allow fear to cause indecision. Focusing on your fears will assure a bad outcome. Manage those fears by weighing the options. Ask yourself what outcome you wish to achieve and what you have to do to achieve this outcome.....while considering that you may not achieve that goal if you don't take a chance. That is, if you don't jump.

Failure to make a decision is not the same thing as making a decision. Simply sitting by while a situation unfolds is not decision making. It represents one of the worst things that a person in a decision making position can do. That course of action (inaction) prevents that person from exerting any influence on the outcome and even increases the probability that a bad outcome will result.

Procrastination can have the same result. Sometimes when a person doesn't want to make a decision that person will delay a decision with the explanation that he is waiting for more information. Gathering information is important and good information is even better but once you have gathered enough information, you should make a decision. After some point, more and more information becomes meaningless because it doesn't change the basic facts upon which a decision is made.

We are all eagles in some way. We cannot let fear and indecision prevent us from taking action. If you really want to be an eagle, trust in yourself, your preparation and your experience, and.......just jump.

Don Wynn

Cool
Calm
Collected

If you were in the hospital await-
ing some serious surgical pro-
cedure, what sort of demeanor
would you want to see in your
doctor? Would the doctor inspire
confidence if she always seemed nervous, distracted, or in a
hurry? Of course not! She would scare her patients just when
they need to be the most relaxed, confident and comfortable.

Consultants are not medical doctors and are not going to remove, rearrange or otherwise affect any body parts. However,
your work is serious and it has serious implications for your
clients! Millions of dollars can be at stake and the careers of
project sponsors can be at risk if projects fail. There is a high
degree of tension inherent in the projects that you work on.

Clients expect consultants they have hired to bring knowledge,
experience and stability to their projects. They can reasonably expect you to plan carefully, test thoroughly, anticipate
potential problems and put measures into place to avoid those
problems. Consultants understand that unexpected things
sometimes happen. When those things happen, professional
consultants respond appropriately and work to resolve each
issue. The client believes you promised success when you entered into the contract and that you will deliver on that promise.

The client needs to have faith in you and you need to understand that they are always watching. You must present a demeanor that causes the client to have unwavering faith in you! You would not be a top technology consultant if you were not deserving of that faith!

If you feel stress, keep it away from the client. If you have reservations about some aspect of a project, bring those fears to the attention of your management and do something to address the cause of the issue. Long hours, deadlines and heavy workloads are a part of the career path you have chosen but you cannot appear to be rushed. You must appear to be methodical and confident even when you are in a hurry.

Provide honest assessments to clients and never tell them anything but the truth while maintaining a confident, controlled demeanor. Maintaining control of yourself allows the client to maintain their faith that their project will be successful under your guidance! You want your clients to say to other potential clients, "If you have (insert your name here) on your project, you have the very best!"

Brand Consciousness

If you are courting Toyota for a contract, should you take the prospective client to lunch in a Ford? You might if you wanted to kill the entire deal. The client might see that as an insult if you did. The prospective client might not say anything but will be on alert for any real or perceived slight related to their brand. Or, if it appears you favor their competitor when making purchasing decisions, the prospective client may believe you favor their competitor(s) now.

Large sums of money and tremendous amounts of corporate effort go into brand development and the client pays close attention to that brand. You should, too. A wise consultant should be as conscious of brand as the client is. Find ways to show the client that you value their brand by doing a little pre-meeting research about the company.

This brand consciousness should be reflected in the tools you use, as well as any comments you might make. If your client has a product that you can use in your consulting activities, you should consider acquiring that product before your first visit. If your client makes pens and pencils you should have an ample supply of their pens in your possession. Be sure to show your interest and awareness of your prospective client's brand by asking knowledgeable questions about their product.

Conversely, make sure that you don't have any of their competitors' products on hand. It is a good practice to check through your briefcase or computer bag before your visit. That will help prevent you from making an embarrassing brand error during your meeting.

If your client advertises a product(s), familiarize yourself with their recent advertisements and with their public image. When the opportunity arises, you can mention that you saw a particular ad or make some meaningful comment about a display you noticed in their office.

All of your efforts in this area should be done with stress on honesty. In fact, honesty should be a theme that carries through all of your activities as a consultant. Look for positive things you can say about the products of your client but do not express false sentiments. Do not say anything that you believe is not true. If you have any negative thoughts, remain objective and keep those thoughts to yourself. A perceived falsehood can damage your credibility.

Embrace Change
Don't Fear It

In consulting, we regularly deal with fear of change in our work (see 'Recognize Client Fears'). If fear of change is common with clients and their employees, then why is it so hard for us as consultants to accept change when it affects us directly or when it affects the way that we do things? Doesn't that seem incongruous?

When faced with direct change, we should evaluate the reason for the change, the associated logistical implications and the cost that might accompany it, just like we ask our clients to do. We should be dispassionate as we do that evaluation because emotions can cloud decisions and conclusions. Clients sometimes offer illogical reasons for their resistance when change will affect them. We should avoid the tendency to do the same thing. It is important that we, as consultants, don't resist change when resistance is illogical. Our responses must be better than that.

Improvement is the desired result when change is contemplated but that does not mean that all change will lead to improvement. Consultants need to keep an open mind and carefully evaluate each potential change before recommending that change to the client. You could apply this same logic whenever a change directly affected you or your company.

Consultants should think of themselves as assertive change agents who are capable of fairly evaluating potential changes which promise to bring some needed improvement. Whether those changes apply to a client or to the consultant or the consultant's company makes little difference in the evaluation strategies. Everything can be expected to change over time but it is the job of the consultant to separate the positive changes from the fads.

Once the consultant's written evaluation has been presented to the client, the consultant's job is to provide objective clarification when requested. Following the client's decision, the consultant should accept and support the client's decision to implement or not implement that contemplated change.

Cookie
Cutter
Solutions

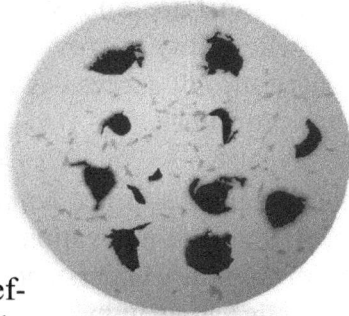

If the solution to the problems you, as a consultant, are asked to solve for your clients could simply be taken directly from reference books they wouldn't need you because clients have bright, capable employees who can read reference books as well as you can. A consultant's greatest value to a client is in those cases where 'one size fits all' solutions are not possible; when the solutions are not simple; when people with average skills cannot solve the problem.

Consultants are called upon when the problems are complex and when the degree of difficulty is high, sometimes when it is extreme. Consultants are most needed when factors combine in unique ways to make the problem more difficult. You are called upon when the client needs the very best!

As a consultant, you and your company will be more successful if you can solve the problems that don't have cookie cutter solutions. How have you done that?

In popular culture, there is a phrase for the ability to avoid cookie cutter solutions. It is called 'thinking outside of the box' but the real name for this quality is innovation. Innovative solutions don't simply follow some predefined and well-known path. Complex, unique problems require innovative solutions that are tailored to the specific nuances of the problem. The ability to provide innovative solutions is one of the cornerstones of success as a consultant and should be one of your core values.

Innovation doesn't just happen. It requires a mindset that is oriented toward innovation. It requires that you put effort and energy into fully understanding the problem. It requires broad knowledge and a willingness to take calculated risks. In some consulting companies simply suggesting an unorthodox, innovative solution can be risky. At the best companies you are expected to consider and evaluate all possible solutions even when the solution is unorthodox. Consultants don't take risks with the result but they do take risks by suggesting unusual solutions. The best consultants brainstorm openly with their fellow technology consultants and freely discuss options that might provide a solution.

Deep knowledge in a particular area may not necessarily foster innovation because it can cause you to stick with 'tried and true' solutions that might not fit the current problem. In order for people with deep knowledge to be innovative they have to make a conscious effort to look at problems from new and different perspectives. Consultants should try to remain conscious of this pitfall and realize that the best solution may require a new approach, a departure from the norm.

Cookie cutter solutions may be a perfect fit for routine problems but if they don't a consultant must be able to draw upon their knowledge and experience to develop innovative solutions. This broad base of knowledge, experience and ability

Don Wynn

to brainstorm with other professional consultants are essential consulting tools. Sometimes applying these tools to solve one problem brings to light the solution for a different problem.

Everyone who works as a consultant should have deep knowledge in one or more areas and broad knowledge across a particular area of technology and across the entire IT industry in general. You need to leverage your knowledge and experience to continue delivering innovative solutions for your clients.

Break It Down
Without Being Insulting

You are an expert at what you do! The management at the client company believes that or they would not have contracted with you or with your company. Most of the employees at the client think that too. Even if they don't think that, they hope it is true because a lot of their success depends on your knowledge, skills and experience.

Part of what proves your expert status is your ability to effectively transfer knowledge to client managers and their employees. Consultants are educators to a great extent. We train the employees of our clients. We sometimes teach formal classes but we are engaged in a training effort even when not in a classroom setting. The hard part for a technology consultant is to gauge the level of knowledge that client employees already have and to execute on the knowledge transfer promise at the right pace and starting at the right level.

If you start at a level that is well below the knowledge that the client employees already have they can react negatively. They may even be insulted. A person might respond by saying, "I am the DBA here! Do you really believe that I don't know what a relational database is"?

If you start at a level that is too advanced you risk confusing the prospective student. Then, if you are lucky, they may say, "Wait a minute, I didn't understand that. Could you repeat it"? If you are not so lucky, they may not say anything even though they did not understand your explanation.

In order to start at the right level, you can ask questions like, "What do you understand about XYZ," or maybe, "What would you like me to explain about XYZ"? It is critical that you listen to employees and that you understand them and their educational needs. The technology you and your consulting company are installing at the client company won't be utilized to its full potential unless the client employees who must use the system after you leave are adequately trained.

Since knowledge transfer sessions are generally centered on solving some problem, you should relate the information provided back to the problem. For example, you might say, "This caused the problem and this is why," before going into a detailed explanation. You could also say, "I am recommending that you take this corrective action and this is why," before providing the explanation.

If you can start knowledge transfer at the appropriate level, your time will be more effectively spent and client employees will be appreciative. The people being trained will voice their appreciation to their management and to you. Your standing as an expert will increase, and you will be much more effective as a consultant.

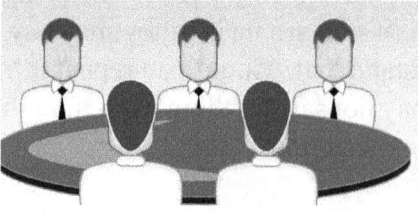

Manage Client Expectations

It may seem that you always get the hard jobs. The challenge you have been handed may be a problem created by a previous consulting company. Tables are corrupted and systems are on the verge of collapse and you have been tasked to provide disaster recovery services. Perhaps, you or your company has built a business reputation based upon providing this type of emergency such repair services. It is not easy work. There are no easy assignments! Even though you possess outstanding skills, success may not be guaranteed if the disaster scenario has progressed too far before you are called upon.

In these situations, the client may not actually expect a miracle but they certainly need one! This client needs good news and you want to give that good news to them. Following a failed technology project, the client will grasp at any positive message. As a professional consultant you must deliver a realistic assessment of the situation and report what can be done to bring a positive result. Manage the expectations of your clients!

Separate emotion from the equation, simply report facts and make recommendations. Concentrate on results that can be supported when devising a project timeline or describing an outcome. Do not simply report what your client wants to hear.

Don Wynn

Some unscrupulous consultants do that already. Those consultants may impress the client initially but the favorable impression quickly fades when the promises and projections are not fulfilled.

Verbal communications can be misinterpreted, and since verbal exchanges are not scripted in advance, it is harder to manage content. Deliver your findings in a written document. Utilize the experience of other consultants on your team to provide input in assessing the work to be done and the amount of time it will take to complete it. Review the written reports and other communications prior to distribution to the client.

Consultants should understand that over-zealous statements can lead to unrealistic client expectations. Avoid describing 'best case' scenarios because those scenarios are not described as 'best case' without reason. 'Best case' scenarios seldom come true and you would be making a mistake if you allow your client to expect that type of outcome. If you allow your client to expect 'best case' results and you deliver a result that is good but not 'best case,' the client may look upon your work as disappointing because it was less than expected. The client may feel that the work took longer and cost more than it should have.

If, on the other hand, you help your client anticipate a realistic result and you are able to deliver a 'best case' result, then their impression of you and your company increases. Regardless of the scope and complexity of the individual job, the client judges the consultant's skills, and that of the consultant's company, based upon how well their expectations are met!

The Best Prepared Usually Wins

'All the consultant does is: show up, fix the problem and then they are done.' This could be the biggest misperception common to non-consultants. Overlooked is the tremendous level of education, preparation, past, present and future, required to become a top consultant. What it takes to remain a top consultant who is competitive in today's market is also underappreciated by those not in consulting. The best technology consultants recognize that changes in technology evolve at a rapid pace, and that staying abreast of current changes while anticipating future trends is paramount to success and longevity in consulting.

Peyton Manning may arguably be the greatest quarterback to ever play professional football. He has a lot of natural ability but that ability was not enough to propel him to the top of his profession. He applied himself in a very conscientious way to develop himself to the greatest extent possible. His preparation allowed him to fully exploit every ounce of potential that he had. Other quarterbacks have entered professional football with similar skills but they never reached the level that Peyton Manning reached. He reached the top of his profession because he understood the need to work and to prepare.

In this way, technology consulting is like professional football

Don Wynn

because the more effort that you put into preparation, the better chance of success you will have. Peyton Manning prepares intensely for the next game and rarely encounters a situation that he has not prepared himself for. Top technology consultants prepare for the next day, for the next meeting, for the next task and for the next project just like Peyton Manning does.

Clients expect expert knowledge and cutting edge skills from their consultants and they will not settle for anything less than that. Since they are paying expert level rates, they should be getting a consultant with expert level skills. The best technology consultants prepare for the future with dedication and intensity. That intense preparation helps them deliver high quality service to their clients.

Knowledge doesn't come through osmosis, and you do not build a solid foundation simply because you work as a consultant every day. You might become good at what you do for that day, or for that year, but you will lose your competitive ability for future projects if you do not continuously study and stay abreast what is going on in your industry. The best consultants know that knowledge and expertise do not come easily. They perform the work expected of them while maintaining a habit of ongoing study. They study topics relating to their current project(s) while trying to obtain insight and understanding of information pertinent in future work. Top consultants understand that the time and effort applied to study is actually an investment in themselves and rather than ease up after they join the ranks of working consultants, top consultants continue their study efforts throughout their career. Knowledge is power and a consultant's education never stops.

Let Me............
Introduce Myself

Consultants sometimes find themselves in the awkward position where they have to introduce themselves. When that happens, you shouldn't stumble or have to search for words. This is such a common event that consultants should know exactly what they will say. Be sure to state your name and company along with the most significant things about yourself. "Hello, my name is Joe Consultant; I am a technology consultant at XYZ Consulting Company. We are an Information Technology Consulting Company specializing in PeopleSoft and Oracle projects." The idea is not that you should say exactly these words but you should always have something in mind for that type of occasion.

Some people find it difficult to mention their positive traits or to mention their successes. It is considered to be in poor taste or even ill-mannered if you do that. We are taught and conditioned to have manners. Talking about your accomplishments seems like bragging and we are taught to be modest as children. We would much prefer to have someone else say positive things about us than to promote ourselves.

However, in this context, talking about yourself is not bragging, it is simply telling the audience about your selling points. It is telling them some of the things that make you and your company a worthy partner on their upcoming projects. Would

Don Wynn

Toyota sell any cars if they did not promote them? As a successful consultant, you have plenty of project experience and should let your clients and prospective clients know about them. If the situation allows you to elaborate, add meaningful information that will present you and your company in a positive light. For example, you could say, "My Company was awarded a contract with the House of Representatives in Washington, D.C., to upgrade their internal computer system. That project will start shortly." or "I recently completed a project for XYZ Company. That project was delivered under budget and on time!"

Of course, to make these statements or assertions, you must stay aware of events that are happening within your company. Both you and your company share the responsibility of timely communication. Staying informed about your company while traveling can be challenging but cell phones and email are a perfect solution.

Just don't go away from a first meeting with someone thinking about what you should have said. Think about it in advance and introduce yourself right when given the opportunity.

Setting the Stage

When a technology consultant goes to a new client they are most often introduced to the project manager and to client employees by a fellow technology consultant. When it is your turn to introduce other consultants you have a great opportunity to set the stage. Providing some professional information in the introduction about the incoming consultant(s) can build their professional standing and sends a message of confidence to the client, as well as to other consultants.

Client managers and employees, several of whom may have seen some of your resumes, will be eager to receive a message of confidence further affirming that your consultants are some of the best in the industry, and that they have made the right decision in hiring you and your company for their project. Clients have high expectations regarding your abilities and thoughtful introductions can further highlight to the client that they have made the right decision.

When introducing someone, use more than his or her name and specialty. It is easy to just say, "This is Joe Consultant, he is a functional consultant working with financials." That is a good start but you can do a little better. After the basic introduction, you could add, "Joe just finished a project for the City of L.A." Then you can redirect to Joe by asking, "Isn't

Don Wynn

that the largest PeopleSoft Financials implementation in North America"? Joe could then respond with a brief description of his work on that project. The whole conversation could take just a few minutes and could provide a good starting point for Joe.

Consultants should make a point to learn things about fellow consultants which can be used when making such introductions. Casual information can be included in the introduction, like where the person is from, where they went to college, a hobby, special vacation or something else that is interesting but the primary focus should be on their respective professional accomplishments, and on your company's accomplishments as a whole.

Consultants are collectively pretty impressive people and have accomplished some impressive things as individuals. Your company's accomplishments are impressive, highlight those accomplishments whenever practical. By being more descriptive during introductions you can share information which might not otherwise be known to the client, thereby enhancing the image of your colleagues and that of your company. The client always wants to believe his company has made the right decision in selecting you and your company for the job.

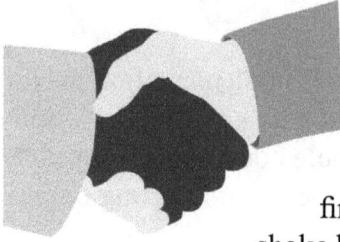

A Good Handshake

When meeting someone for the first time, it is usually appropriate to shake hands but is a handshake reserved for the first time you meet someone? Well, maybe not. You can shake hands in many different scenarios. It probably wouldn't be appropriate to shake someone's hand at the start of a meeting when you work with him or her every day. However, it is usually appropriate if you see that person occasionally. A good handshake goes a long way to create a cordial business relationship.

A firm, confident handshake is important. A handshake is not a contest. It is not a demonstration of dominance or deference. It is simply a greeting. Do not try to crush the other person's hand. You are not arm wrestling. You are just trying to introduce yourself to someone. Fully engage the other person's hand, don't just shake with your fingers. Being too weak is as bad as being too strong. A 'Weak Fish' handshake is uncomfortable for the person receiving your hand.....this applies to both men and women.

A good firm handshake provides the opening for a business relationship to get started in a positive way but there is more going on than just the handshake. Make eye contact as you shake hands, listen carefully to the other person's name and repeat it to make sure you heard it correctly.

If you have a problem with sweaty palms, dust your hands lightly with powder prior to your meeting. Gold Bond mois-

Don Wynn

ture control powder works very well and doesn't have the tell-tale aroma that baby powder does.

In the first few seconds following the handshake, engage in a friendly conversation but avoid any sort of topic that could be divisive. A lot of business people follow sports in the cities where they work. For example, if you were in New York, you might say, "Are you a baseball fan, Yankees or Mets?" That should cause some sort of banter about sports in the city.

If someone approaches you to introduce themselves, you should always stand to face them whenever possible. And this is not just a 'man thing.' Women should also stand when being introduced to a man or a woman. You know the rest of the routine: smile, give a firm handshake, look them in the eye, state your name and repeat their name back to them.

On Time, Every Time

Professionals are consistent and predictable. They always act the same. They have set personal standards for their professional conduct and seldom deviate from those standards. If you want to be viewed as a professional by your clients and colleagues, you should act professionally adhere to set professional standards.

One important standard is to be timely. If you are supposed to be in a meeting, always be on time. If you are to be on a conference call, be on time. If you have some document or other work that is due, be on time. If you have any sort of professional activity scheduled, it is very important to be on time.

At the same time, it is important not to be too early. If you always arrive for meetings early, it can give the impression that you don't have enough to do. The client may begin to wonder, "Are we paying Joe just to sit around"? Your challenge is to be on time without being too early.

Things happen that you cannot control and cannot predict. If something happens that will cause you to be late or to miss a deadline, let the people who will be affected know about the delay. Tell them why the delay occurred and let them know when you will arrive or when the late task will be completed. You should always provide as much advance notice as you can. If you know on Friday that you will be late for a meeting on Monday, you should notify the chairman of the meeting on Friday.

Consistency and predictability are key traits of professionals.

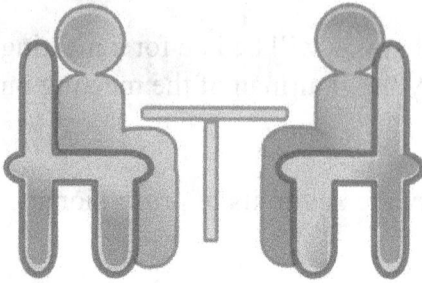

Where Do I Sit?

It may seem silly but your choice of a seat is important when you attend meetings! The person who conducts the meeting is probably the Project Leader and will likely occupy the seat at the head of the conference table. That position allows every participant to see the leader and gives the leader a position of power in the meeting. If you arrive early and the seat at the head of the table is vacant, do not sit there unless you are the lead in that meeting or unless the leader is already there and seated in another seat.

The role you expect to play in the meeting still determines where you should sit even if you are not the meeting leader. If you are an Area Lead at the client site, you should sit as close to the meeting leader as you can. From this position, you can interact with the meeting leader more effectively and are in a position to represent your ideas and your company more effectively.

If you are a support player on the team you should select a seat as they are available at the table. Defer your seating choice to client employees, especially if those client employees can reasonably be expected to play a significant part in the meeting. Extra seats sometimes line the outside walls of the conference room which you might choose if you do not expect to play a significant role in that meeting.

Don Wynn

Project Leaders should avoid sitting in the seats lining the wall unless every other seat is taken. If you are not a Lead but expect to be asked to play an active part in the meeting, try not to sit in these seats because it causes people at the table to stretch their necks or turn around when you speak. Meeting participants need to see you in order to clearly hear and understand what you say. However, sitting in the 'cheap seats' does not mean that you are free to disengage from the discussion. Pay attention and participate when appropriate. If you do have something to contribute to the meeting, do not let your seat at the back or along the sides of the room affect you. Speak up when you have a positive contribution.

If the conference table happens to be round....... you are on your own!

Sit Up & Pay Attention

My elementary school teachers must have said, "Sit up and pay attention," to me a million times during that period of my life. Like most young kids, I think I was always fidgeting and moving around in my seat. My teachers may have suspected that I would eventually become a technology consultant because that advice is especially pertinent in the consulting profession! In fact, it is probably true for almost any profession.

When in a meeting or conference room your posture makes an impression and sends a message. Sit up, lean forward toward the table rather than back and away from it; pay attention, make eye contact with the speaker and participate in the conversation when appropriate. This causes the other people in the room to have a more positive impression of you and of your contribution to the meeting.

Avoid slouching, crossing your arms on your chest, leaning back in your chair and constantly checking your watch or the wall clock! If you are taking notes, avoid the temptation to doodle in the margins of your notepad. When taking notes, you should make sure that you don't simply stare at your note pad without ever looking at the other participants. All of these activities convey lack of interest and boredom! That is definitely not the impression you want to give.

Don Wynn

Body language, posture and facial expressions speak volumes! Sitting back in your chair with your arms crossed can impart an impression of hostility or arrogance. Both of these impressions can affect how the meeting progresses as well as how other people in the meeting respond to you.

Holding your hands in front of or even near your mouth when speaking can make it hard for people in the meeting to hear you when you speak. If they cannot hear you they could easily misinterpret or misunderstand what you say. The best approach is to keep your hands on the table or at your side.

Side conversations and talking over others are very disrespectful to other participants in the meeting and especially to the chairman. Wait for an opening in the conversation or for acknowledgement from the chairman before speaking, then address to the entire group.

New opportunities for rude behavior also exist. If you have your laptop, PDA or smart phone with you avoid the urge to check your messages.....and, just like in the movies, put your phone on vibrate. Sending e-mail or messages during meetings is equally distracting and rude. Surfing the web is an especially egregious act and should be completely out of the question!

Chewing gum is usually not appropriate in any business setting while drinking or eating might be acceptable if that is the norm for the company.

If you arrive late for the meeting, quietly take a seat and apologize for your tardiness. Avoid disrupting the meeting as much as you can. If you need to leave the room before the meeting is over, wait for a pause in the discussion, if possible. Try to avoid leaving the room while someone is speaking. When you do leave, simply exit the room with as little fanfare as possible. If you know that you will have to leave the meeting early, it is good manners to notify the chairman prior to the start of the meeting that you will be leaving and the time you plan to leave. Ask if any topics that might require your input to be handled early in the meeting so you can fully participate.

It is not hard to make a good impression in meetings but it is also very easy to make a bad impression if you fail to follow some common sense rules as guides for your behavior.

Mrs. Webb, my 3rd grade teacher, really was a smart woman!

Don Wynn

Concentrate on Listening Before Speaking

Listen carefully before speaking. There are several reasons for taking that approach. First, you need to have all the available information before offering an opinion or possible solution to any problem. Listening engages the person who is speaking and shows respect for their input. Listening builds the sense of team.

It is human nature to ascribe credibility to people who do not speak all the time. That is especially true if they make thoughtful and accurate comments when they do speak. Clients value consultants who actually listen to them and who take their opinions and input seriously. Your clients have that trait just as strongly as everyone else does!

A person who carefully listens and then speaks after having done so often has more credibility than someone who speaks too frequently or too quickly!

An additional benefit is that it is not uncommon for some solution to become apparent by carefully listening to the description of the problem; the solution just seems to develop itself. If not, the team may be able to resolve the issue by collaboratively discussing what the client has described.

In my career, I have many examples of where careful listening to a problem led to a solution. At one point, I was a senior design engineer working for one of the first companies in the Cad-Cam (computer aided design and computer aided manufacturing) arena. One of my responsibilities was to conduct tours of our facilities for important customers. On one of those tours, I told the group that we were unable to make use of robotic equipment to place components on our circuit boards because our components were so close to one another. Our equipment had a clearance problem. One of the people in the group I was escorting asked, "Can't you use the robot to install every other component"? That solution had never occurred to us and was only possible because the person was concentrating on listening and on understanding the problem. Implementing that simple idea eliminated a major production bottleneck for the company.

Speaking too quickly can lead to mistakes and can make you appear impetuous. Those mistakes will diminish your credibility in the eyes of the client. It is better to hold your input until you have a full understanding of the problem. Your input at that point will be more meaningful.

Don't Trash Past Clients or Other Consultants

One of the most important things that technology consultants bring to their projects is experience with similar problems at similar companies. That experience is one of the factors that make us valuable to our clients. An added positive factor is that we are not going through the process for the first time and we are not trainees.

Every project is not a positive experience but all projects provide experience in one way or another. Consultants build upon that experience in order to provide value for their clients. For example, you may learn that there are certain things that should not be done in specific situations even though those things may look like good options. You may learn that some simple tasks are much more important to be done than might be apparent.

It is not uncommon for clients to require consultants to sign non-disclosure agreements before being allowed to begin work on their projects. Those agreements limit the things that you can say about former clients but your personal approach to your profession should limit your comments even further than that.

It is generally a good policy to avoid naming past clients

when giving examples and it is wise to avoid criticism that could be offensive. Careful wording can make a lot of difference. You could say things like 'we tried this at one of my past clients and it did not work well. Let me tell you why….' rather than 'ABC Company did that even though I told them that it would be a stupid thing to do. They got what they deserved…' Always keep in mind that whatever success the client has, you are a team member and are a part of that. The same is true when the client has a less positive result. Consultants share the credit for success but also share the blame for less successful projects.

The question for all consultants is how do you reference your past experience so that the current client understands that you base your input on an entire set of experiences?

The most important thing to remember is that you should be able to explain the 'cause and effect' of actions. If some action caused a negative impact at one of your past clients and if your current client is planning to take a similar action, you should explain your experience without divulging the name of the past client.

A corollary to this concept is that it is better to avoid criticism of other consultants or of other consulting companies. If a client is critical of other consultants and other companies, that carries weight and could have an impact on your future. If you do that, it could invite unwanted comparisons and could make you seem petty. You could say something like 'I don't understand why this was done this way. If I had been here, I might have done it the same way if I were faced with the same circumstances.' Statements like that will cause the client to begin questioning past actions but will not be seen as direct criticism.

Don Wynn

Time Management

'Time is money' like the old adage says. You are asked to manage time in many different areas of your work. You manage deliverables and timelines but you also manage meetings and daily activities. The way that you meet your time management obligations affects the way clients perceive you.

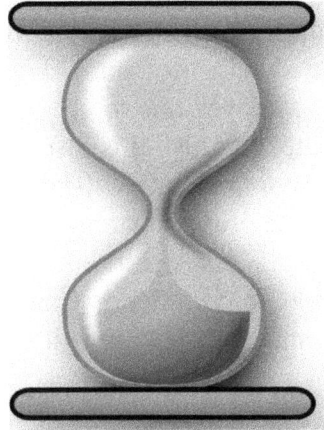

Time spent in meetings is very valuable but, if spent capriciously, it can be a drain on the resources of the client and the project. If you serve as the chairperson for a meeting, start the meeting on time. It reflects poorly upon you as an individual and your company if scheduled meetings are allowed to start after the announced start time. If you are an attendee but are not the chairperson make sure that you are in the meeting room ready for the meeting to start on time.

Client employees, especially those who have budgetary responsibilities, often begin calculating the cost in real dollars of meeting delays. Meetings with large numbers of participants can easily cost thousands of dollars in fees. These costs are not lost on the people who must attend project steering committee meetings where they discuss the ongoing costs and benefits of your projects.

Ending meetings on time is equally important! If you are the chairperson and it seems certain that a meeting will exceed the allotted time, you should say, "It is clear that we need more time to cover this topic. Can you extend the meeting by 30 minutes to finish this discussion or do you need to schedule a follow-up meeting"? The decision should be made with input from the group of attendees. Any decision to extend a meeting or to schedule a follow-up meeting should be made before the scheduled completion time. It is important to avoid running over the scheduled meeting time before making this decision.

Of course, a decision to extend the meeting should consider the availability of the meeting room. It is inappropriate and discourteous to extend a meeting or to run over the scheduled completion time if the result is that you inconvenience the next meeting scheduled in that room.

Start on time, stop on time, respect everyone's time and make a positive impression!

Freshman Mistakes

Can you remember your freshman year in high school or college? If so, you might recall feeling somewhat awkward. Everyone seemed to know where they were going but you. Everything was new and a little strange at the same time. You probably didn't know the routine, where anything was......you simply did not know the 'drill.' The simplest things offered a challenge, like the location of the library, or that in high school freshman must never use the senior lunch line or sit at certain tables or which bus to take home. Freshmen just can't help themselves, they just don't know any better. The desire to prove themselves and the lack of knowledge combined can cause freshmen to make simple mistakes that have large consequences.

If the desire to impress the client, or other consultants, leads to a display of bravado, you are setting the groundwork to make a 'freshman mistake.' That is the term I use when everyone in the room or in the discussion knows that you have made a mistake but you don't know it. Freshman mistakes are not the exclusive province of the young, older consultants often make such blunders when trying too hard to impress. Freshman mistakes destroy your personal credibility almost immediately. Once someone begins to think of you as a freshman or as a junior consultant, you may never be able to regain your status as an expert at that client site. The impact of making a freshman mistake can be profound and long lasting.

If you realize that you have made a mistake, acknowledge it and move on. Once a mistake has been made, one of the worst things you can do is to continue to defend the mistake or to insist that there was no mistake.

Trust your judgment but understand your limits at the same time. Resist the urge to suggest that some long-standing problem at the client site is really very simple and that it will be easily resolved. Don't promise solutions until you are absolutely certain that you can deliver on your commitments. Everyone wants to impress clients with their value and knowledge. Don't let that desire to impress cause you to offer possible solutions too quickly.

Professors may not expect much from freshmen but clients always expect Doctorate level knowledge and skill from their consultants. The client believes they hired an expert. Don't allow your desire to prove yourself cause you to make a 'freshman mistake' and cause the client to change their mind about you and your skills.

What's Fair Is Fair

The general goal of the expense statement is to be fair to everyone involved. When working under expenses accounts the objective is not to pad the income of consultants.

Expense statements are a routine component of the technology consulting industry. Tremendous amounts of money may be involved and disagreements can result. Opinions are formed based upon expense account entries. Those opinions may never be vocalized but they can definitely affect the work of consultants.

Maybe the technology consultant can reduce the chance that stress will result from disagreements about expense account entries if they define what is expected at the outset of the project. Adopt a set of personal rules that can be followed when considering items to be submitted.

The most important thing to do is to think about what the expense account is supposed to do. It is supposed to cover travel expenses related to your travel and to your work. It is supposed to prevent the consultant from having out of pocket expenses as a result of their work and provides a way for the client to cover the consultant's routine and normal expenses.

The basic rule I have followed for many years is that I will evaluate an expense item by comparing it to personal travel. I ask myself, "If I were paying for this from my own money, would I do it"? If the answer is yes, then I believe it is appropriate to include the expense on an expense statement.

One approach that can be used to minimize disagreements about expense account entries is to use the per diem rates that are established by the U.S. government. That prevents to consultant from spending too much time collecting receipts and preparing expense account entries.

Another approach is the use of 'bundled rates'. Under this approach, the client agrees to pay a set amount per hour to cover the travel related costs for consultants…..and collecting receipts is no longer necessary. The 'bundled rate' amount should be calculated to cover the things that would normally be covered on expense statements and simplifies expense calculation and reporting for both the consultant and the payroll department.

Regardless of how expense statements are handled, it is important to avoid conflict about expense account entries.

Don Wynn

Advisors to the King

Decisions can be made in many different ways. The important thing for consultants to remember is that the client makes the decision we only get to make recommendations. That may be very hard to accept because, after all, we are the experts. Why would a client hire us and then ignore our recommendations? We might like to know why a recommendation was ignored but the client might not be willing to tell us.

In a manner of speaking the client is the King and the consultant is a trusted advisor. Once we have made a recommendation to the King and after we have explained the reasoning for our recommendation, our obligation is finished. The King doesn't have any obligation to follow that recommendation once he has listened to our recommendation and to our logic. The King may choose to offer an explanation but as often as not, the King will make a decision without further discussion.

When I became a consultant, a lawyer friend told me that I would not like it. He told me that I would have to make a very strong adjustment. I failed to understand until he explained, "You will have the same problem I have. I can meet with a client to discuss a legal issue. I can explain their options and recommend a particular course of action. I can also advise them regarding a possible bad outcome should they decline to act on my recommendations. Then the client pays my fee and leaves. In a few months, the client returns to ask me to help resolve the problems that were caused because the client failed to heed my warning, and failed to follow my original recommendation. Accordingly, my ability to help with the client's problem has been made more challenging and time consuming, and the client's costs escalate." My lawyer friend was very frustrated but described this scenario as pretty common. Consultants are somewhat like lawyers in that we are engaged to make recommendations. Consultants do not make decisions. Sometimes, those decisions coincide with our recommendations and sometimes they do not.

It really doesn't matter what the reasons are behind the decision. We should realize that our client, the King, must suffer the consequences of that decision whether the outcome good or bad. Our recommendation may be just one source of input that the King gets during the decision making process. There may be underlying factors that go into the King's decision that extend beyond the arguments that we have offered.

But in the end, the King wields the sword and makes the decisions.

Never Surprise
With Bad News

It is just human nature to want to provide good news and to avoid delivering bad news. That desire can cause consultants to make a serious mistake in terms of service to clients. If we avoid or delay delivering bad news, we may take away or diminish the opportunity that the client might have had to resolve the problem. By taking decisive action early enough, the problem may be able to be avoided all together.

In my experience, the worst fear of most program managers is that something bad will happen and they will not be able to resolve it. Worse yet is a program manager's fear that he will be the last one to know about the problem, and then have to explain his lack of awareness of that problem to his boss. The manager is due the courtesy of being able to respond as quickly as possible when events occur which might threaten the success of the project.

If the bad news relates directly to an area where the consultant has responsibility, there may be a tendency to try to resolve the problem without involving anyone else and without highlighting the issue. That is the appropriate approach as long as the consultant really can resolve the problem in a reasonable amount of time. If the consultant is simply postponing the inevitable, then it is not appropriate. It is also not appropriate if the consultant has to take short cuts or to do something that they might not ordinarily do. It is definitely not appropriate if the consultant would feel a need to disguise any action that was taken.

When to deliver bad news? If the consultant cannot resolve the issue through accepted methods in a timely manner, that consultant must not delay in notifying the project leadership. Do not wait because there will likely never be a good time. Don't wait until after lunch or until tomorrow. Deliver the bad news to the leadership at the earliest possible moment to allow for the greatest amount of time to correct the problem.

If you delay, the first few questions you will be asked is likely to be, "When did you learn of this problem," and "Why didn't you tell me earlier"? The repercussions will be even more severe than they might otherwise have been had the message been delivered more expediently. There may be repercussions when you deliver bad news regardless of how quickly you do it but that is part of the responsibility that consultants have when they take on assignments. The consultant should be held accountable for actions that they take and for any mistakes they make.

Consultants owe a high level of service to clients and delivering bad news is sometimes what we have to do. Bad news should never be a surprise. A professional consultant should share that information with the client as soon as possible. Good News, on the other hand, is a little different. People always enjoy getting good news and that can be delayed if nothing else depends directly on the result you are reporting. Good news can be a very nice surprise. If you have good news to share, you may wait a few hours or even days, or even a special event to share that news.

Don Wynn

Who Cares About Knowledge Transfer?

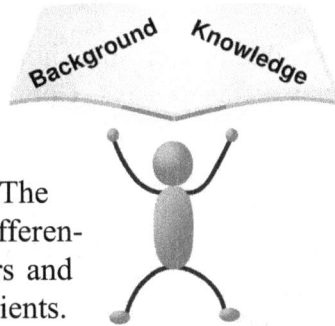

Background Knowledge

Professional technology consultants and their companies care! The best consultants care because it differentiates them from their competitors and increases their value to their clients. They care because it reflects their professionalism and leadership in the industry and represents a fundamental component of good client service.

Clients care about knowledge transfer, too. They care because they realize that a smooth running system is critical to the success of their organizations. Clients also realize that these systems are becoming increasingly more complex as new features and capabilities are added, and that the client's internal staff must be knowledgeable about these comprehensive systems in order to utilize, maintain and support them. What good is a tool if you don't know how to use it?

Client employees care. Employees care because they realize they will be the ones to operate, support and maintain these complex systems in the future. They will be on the front line after that last consultant has departed.......when there may not be day to day consulting support available. Employees care because they need it to be effective in their jobs and because it enhances their personal value to their employer. They care because it helps them develop their skills and enhances their careers.

Consultants can and should provide knowledge transfer in many different ways. Consultants should provide formal training seminars and classes when called upon to do that. They should also provide knowledge transfer in their daily, one-on-one interactions with client employees. Consultants should take a few extra minutes to provide explanations when they perform their daily work. "This is what I have just done and this is why I did it." That type of interaction with client employees will increase the value of the service that you provide and will be noted and appreciated by your client.

Knowledge transfer is a two-way street. Consultants gain knowledge about the client organization by interacting with client employees. They might even gain new insights into creative ways that the software can be setup and used. By acknowledging that you expect to learn from client employees is a team-building thing to do. It will cause client employees to be much more accepting of the consultant who does that.

Knowledge Transfer is important to consultants and to their clients. You should continue to embrace it and you should use the phrase 'knowledge transfer' liberally in your communications so that the client understands that you are consciously doing that.

Build Credibility Even When You Don't Know the Answer

Clients are like children in one significant way. They are like children because they constantly watch and evaluate. They pay attention to everything consultants do even when they don't seem to be paying attention to anything. Every action of a consultant either builds credibility or damages it.

Clients expect consultants to bring specific knowledge and experience to their projects. They expect consultants to be able to answer their detailed questions regardless of the improbability or obscurity of the question. Consultants typically utilize their experience and do a very good job of answering client questions. Every time a consultant answers a question correctly, credibility is built in the eyes of the client.

Clients have faith in the skills of the consultant before they select a consultant for their project. Faith in your consulting skills is typically based upon your resume, references and the interview. That initial faith is limited and will grow or diminish as the project progresses. The client's trust and faith in the consultant grows every time one of the client's questions is answered correctly. Client trust in the consultant grows and valuable credibility is gained.

What happens when the client asks a question that the consultant cannot answer? What impact does that have on the credibility of the consultant? Well, the answer to those questions depends almost completely on the responses to the questions. Answering incorrectly will damage the consultant's credibility and potentially could destroy it. The accuracy of that incorrect answer might not be known for some time but when it is learned that the answer was wrong, the consultant's credibility will suffer. This is especially true if the client makes decisions based on the consultant's incorrect answer. The message here is to never guess.

If a consultant does not know the answer, the consultant should acknowledge that they don't know it. That simple acknowledgement maintains credibility because it is honest and people appreciate and respect honesty. Explaining that the question or problem is outside your area of expertise will not damage your credibility but making an incorrect guess surely will. Guessing is in sharp conflict with the requirement to always be honest with the client.

Once the consultant has acknowledged that they don't know the answer, there are several options. The consultant can just let it drop.....but that is the worst option. Or the consultant can refer the client that another member of the consulting team who is more knowledgeable in the area in question, providing that team member actually does have more expertise and experience in the area in question. The consultant can also relate the client's question to an area where the consultant is familiar. For example, "Your question is about Financials and I am not as familiar with Financials as I am with Supply/Chain

Don Wynn

but there is a similar feature in Supply/Chain that works like this…" Then offer to put the client in touch with the team member who is better qualified to address the client's question.

Can anyone know all the answers? The client may seem to expect that but that is an irrational expectation because it is impossible for a single person to know all the answers. Some consultants come very close but they still don't know everything. Consultants bring deep knowledge and professionalism to their work. They know a lot of the answers and have the resources behind them to find answers for the ones they don't know.

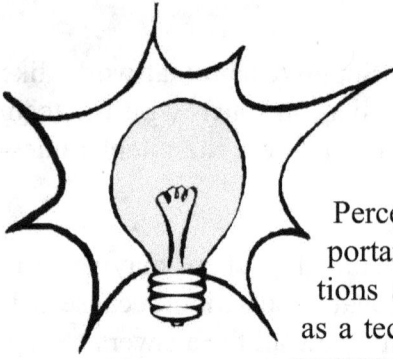

Whose Idea Was That?

Perception is important and it is important to understand how perceptions are formed. When you work as a technology consultant at a client company, you frequently work with the employees of the client as teammates or as support staff. These client employees usually have some preconceived notions about consultants and their place in the world.

One common perception is that consultants will simply repeat some idea that they heard from client employees who are knowledgeable about the issues at the client site. Client employees almost always expect consultants to take credit for those ideas and, as a result, are sometimes reluctant to share vital information or their opinions. Since most technology consulting has a collegial component, it is important to minimize that type of perception by client employees. It is just a basic rule of business ethics to give credit for ideas to the people who originated those ideas.

To some people, a consultant is simply a 'thief with a laptop'; someone who makes more money than they are worth and who cannot possibly know the specific nuances of the problems at the client company. To the doubters, the consultant is just someone who is overpaid, has unproven worth, comes in claiming expert status, and will claim credit in the end for everything good that happens even when they have not earned it. Take heart, not every client employee thinks this way. For every one doubter you encounter, you will also encounter ten appreciative and admiring employees who are eager to learn from and help you. Now, all you have to do is make allies out of the doubters.

A professional technology consultant is aware of the importance of perception and will do things that should improve perceptions. For example, if some idea came up during a conversation with an employee of the client company, it is crucial to acknowledge the contribution of that client employee. You could say something like, "Joe Client and I were talking about this last week and he suggested that I look at this as a possible solution. That turned out to be a very good idea."

Any sort of acknowledgement of the contribution of client employees is a strongly positive thing as long as the comments that you make are true. Do not provide false praise. Clear and objective praise of client employees using their names is a very effective way to change employee perceptions of you. When offering praise, it is best if you can do it in a public place and if you can do it when the client employee can see the e-mail or can hear the comments acknowledging their contribution.

An additional negative perception may be that the consultant is over-compensated for the contribution that they are making. The client employee will not usually know exactly what the consultant is being paid but the perception can be that it is too much, no matter how much it is. A technology consultant can reduce or even eliminate that perception by providing knowledge transfer to client employees.

The message conveyed by the consultant to the client should

be that, "We will work as a team to resolve issues in the best and fastest possible way." That message affirms that the consultant is the expert but realizes and appreciates that everyone on the team has something to offer toward problem resolution and attainment of team goals.

You will increase cooperation and productivity if you spend time explaining why something should be done a certain way rather than just saying, "Do it like this." The client employee will appreciate that approach and may well make comments to others like, "Sam Consultant is the best consultant I have ever worked with." Praise like that is a very powerful message when management hears it from their employees.

Follow Up

Do you know the answer to all the questions and situations that you might encounter in your work? Probably not! In fact, it is most likely impossible for you to know the answer to every possible question. So prepare hard for your work but don't place an unreal expectation on yourself to know everything. That will add stress to your life without increasing your effectiveness.

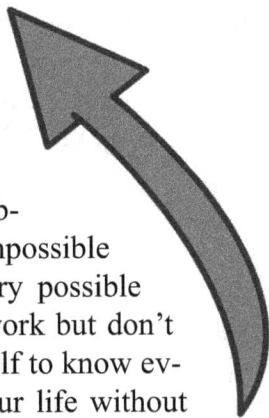

Follow Up is an important thing to remember. A professional technology consultant will provide follow up information to the questions that they are asked directly. That just seems to make sense and most people will do it automatically. The aspect of follow up that some people miss is that they fail to elaborate after the original question is asked and after the original answer has been given.

It is not uncommon for a consultant to recall some additional facts after they have given their initial answer. When that happens, the additional information can be given verbally when you are speaking with the person who asked the question or at the next meeting where the same people are present. If that is not possible, e-mail or a document should be produced that covers the new information. Consultants cannot allow their clients to ignore or to fail to recognize important information.

Feedback and follow up can and should be provided even if a

specific question was not asked. In other words, you can provide feedback or follow up with additional information as the result of a previous conversation about some topic. You could say, "Yesterday, we had a discussion about....... and I would like to provide some additional information that might also be helpful....."

The most outstanding technology consultants are the most forthcoming with information. Consultants should anticipate the information needs of their clients and provide pertinent information even before the client realizes that they need it! The client simply may not understand that they should ask a specific question or that they should consider some specific element. The best technology consultants use their experience to help guide their clients around and away from potential pitfalls.

You can ask, "Have you considered this situation or this circumstance," or "Can we discuss this issue in more detail"? Those questions can open up discussions where additional information can be provided.

The best solution to a problem is reached when the problem is fully understood by all participants and when all possible alternatives have been identified and discussed. Consultants have a responsibility to make that happen.

What's in a Title?

Titles may seem old fashioned in the modern 'Casual Friday' world. Consultants and everyone else have grown accustomed to addressing people by their first names in business as well as in social settings. Using first names implies a comfort level with the person being addressed and has become the most common way of referring to people.

What about people who have titles associated with their names? How should those people be addressed? Most consultants are not likely to encounter Kings or Queens or Presidents in their work but they may encounter Mayors, Councilmen, Police Chiefs, Fire Chiefs, School Superintendents, various Board Chairmen and other officials of client organizations. Is it still appropriate to address these people using their first names? Casual references may be appropriate in a social setting but they are almost never appropriate in a business relationship, especially in public or in the presence of other employees of the client. This is true in every case unless the person you are addressing has specifically asked the consultant to use their first name, and even then the consultant should defer to a title in a professional setting.

People who have earned titles use them almost exclusively in their business or official capacities. The title is a point of pride for them and recognizes their status within the organization or entity. Mayors are addressed using their title and last name; Councilmen are addressed in the same manner. Other officials and members of the military are addressed using their title or rank.

How do you respond if an official asks us to address them by their first names? For instance, the client company president greets you with, "Welcome. I am happy to meet you, please call me Jim." Even after receiving this friendly invitation you should still use the more formal approach when addressing client company hierarchy when you are in public places and official meetings. The use of first names is more appropriately used in private settings or in small, more relaxed meetings. Use your best professional judgment when addressing officials in public.

Consultants can never make a mistake by using a person's title when addressing them. It is almost always a mistake if consultants seem too familiar by using first names instead of a title when addressing officials in a public setting.

Connect

Consulting is a profession that requires constant communication with a lot of different people at all levels in the client company. It requires interaction with other consultants as well. There are many different channels but the one that is probably used most often is just to talk to people. Consultants might have a hundred short conversations every day but they may only generate a dozen e-mails and a single written document. It is important to make those short verbal exchanges as effective as possible.

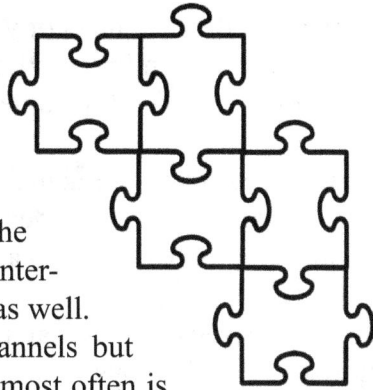

Making eye contact with the people you are speaking to is extremely important. That makes it possible for the consultant to determine if the message is understood. It also shows respect for everyone in the conversation.

When you approach someone and initiate a conversation, it would probably be difficult to avoid eye contact. In that context, you expect eye contact and you almost instinctively look for it. Eye contact is simply one of the non-verbal components of almost any conversation. Body language and facial expression are others.

When someone approaches you, it may not be as natural to make eye contact. If you are busy doing paperwork or working at a computer station, it may be tempting to keep your eyes on the document or on the screen. You may not want to lose your place in the document or you may be concentrated on the task at hand. You might participate in en entire conversation without ever looking at the other person.

In that context, you are actually sacrificing two activities at once. Your attention is divided even if you do not look away from the work at hand. Both activities might suffer.

If you cannot look up, you can tell the person who approached you that you will be busy for a few minutes and that you will get back to them. That lets them know that you are not simply ignoring them and prevents you from dividing your attention. When you do that, make sure that you follow up as you told them you would.

If you decide to have the conversation with them at that time, you should get to a point in your work where you can stop. Then you should face the person who initiated the conversation. Sometimes you may have to turn around. Once you are in the conversation, give it your undivided attention.

Avoiding eye contact when you are in a conversation can show hostility or disgust. It can easily be insulting to the other person in the conversation even when no insult is intended. The insult may be even more severe if your back is to the other person.

Making eye contact will improve the quality of your verbal communications.

Don Wynn

What's In A Name?

People like to hear their names. Using a person's name when you address them can build a sense of team and camaraderie, and may facilitate feelings of familiarity and closeness.

Try to use a person's name whenever addressing that person. For example, you might say, "John, what do you think of the report I sent you last night"? In a reciprocal manner, you should encourage them to use your name when they address you. Bear in mind though that the name you use to address that person may be that person's title, especially if that person is high in the client company hierarchy or someone in an official capacity. However, using first names in social settings and everyday work events can imply a sense of friendly inclusiveness. Give thought to how you use this powerful tool.

There aren't many hard rules in sociology but it is as close to a rule as there is that people who work closely together usually gain a growing respect for one another. In a general sense, we tend to become more appreciative of people as we work with them in more and more situations. Simply using the other person's name when working with them can accelerate that process. There are, of course, exceptions to almost any rule.

If you encounter someone whom you find unpleasant or simply annoying for some reason, try to understand and expect that they probably find you equally annoying. In this situation, mutual negative feelings tend to degrade over time. In other words, the situation probably will not improve. Keep all your interactions with that person both short and professional. The other person will appreciate that and you will be much more effective if you follow this recommendation.

If using a person's name is good, is creating a nickname or using an existing nickname better? No, no, no, no, it isn't. Creating a nickname for someone can have very adverse results. That implies a familiarity that may not be welcomed. The nickname may convey something entirely different than you intended. If you repeat a nickname for someone that you heard someone else use, you are really getting into a very unpredictable area. The person referred to by that nickname may not even be aware that other people are referring to them that way and you will be blamed for assigning that nickname.

A professional consultant will avoid using any nickname for a client or for anyone else at the client site because the repercussions are so unpredictable. That same professional consultant will use names in a thoughtful and respectful manner.

Don Wynn

Don't Embarrass the Client

It is a common saying that there is no such thing as a stupid question. That's not true. It simply means that the people who say that have never asked one or that they have never been made to feel that one of their questions was stupid. It is very easy for someone to think that they have asked a stupid question based upon your response to them. You need to be very conscious of the impact that your answer to a question can have.

That consciousness should be even more acute if you are in a group setting. For example, if you are alone with the person who asks 'a less than well thought out' question, you can respond immediately but it might be better if you don't respond so quickly if you are in a group. The reason for the difference is that you can protect the reputation of the person who asked the question with a well-constructed answer.

If you are alone, you can give the answer and explain it without making the person look bad in front of friends and co-workers. When the question is asked, you should easily know if the answer could be seen to make the person who asked it look stupid or foolish. The questioner may also realize that the answer is obvious even before you begin to answer. Even if they don't, you can say things like, "I can understand why you might ask that. I would answer your question this way…" Apply a response that does not ridicule the question to protect your relationship with the person and avoid discouraging them from asking other questions. In this way, you protect the reputation of the person asking the question.

If you are not alone, your answer is even more important because a 'less than well thought answer' could be viewed by the person who asked the question as publically ridiculing them. A terse or seemingly derisive answer will not only serve to embarrass that person but will also be noted by others present and may reduce their likelihood of asking many questions in the future for fear of being publically embarrassed.

Playing the 'I'm the expert' card in this situation will not serve you well here. The client already thinks of you as the expert or you would not be there. This situation calls upon your expert social skills and a little compassion. How you respond in this instance can build or undermine your professional credibility and damage how you are perceived as an individual.

You can minimize damage to the questioner's ego and reputation in several ways. The best approach is to avoid answering the question until you can be alone with them. You can say, "I'll get back to you on that," and simply move on. Or you could say, "Can we discuss this later"? You might even say, "I'd like to think about that before answering."

Once you have given the answer, the person will probably realize how the question might have made them look if you had answered differently. You have to have faith that they will appreciate and remember this little kindness. Furthermore, even if you believe a question was stupid or foolish, never express that opinion to anyone. Simply let your answer stand for itself.

Don Wynn

That's Just Ridiculous!

Ideas come and ideas go, some of them are worth pursuing and some are not. Some are brilliant, or at least they seem to border on brilliant. Some are just not very good and some may be outright ridiculous.

The question for you is how should you react when each type of idea is offered as the solution to a problem or as a direction that should be taken. The short answer is to listen attentively to every idea. Don't pre-judge any idea because you may simply misunderstand the idea because of the way it was presented. Once the entire idea has been explained, then you can respond.

When you believe an idea is good or even better than that, acknowledge the source of that idea. Recognition is an important thing and everyone on a team needs to get the recognition and credit that they deserve. Taking credit for an idea that was not yours will destroy you in the eyes of the team and is one of the most serious mistakes that a consultant can make.

You don't have to make a formal announcement in order to give credit. You can say something like. "We need to discuss Joe's idea more." You could also say, "Joe, that was a very good idea, we need to elaborate on that to see if it fits." Regardless of what you say, always be truthful. Never try to manufacture a compliment. If a comment is deserved people will know it and they will appreciate it. If a comment is not deserved people will know that too and the response will not be good. Giving false praise will diminish any praise you offer in the future.

When you believe an idea or suggestion is not good or even bordering on the ridiculous, you should resist the urge to say, "That's just ridiculous!" A blunt response like that would be insulting and could set the tone for your relationship for the entire project with the person who offered it. It could also cause that person, as well as others who overheard your response, to hold back in later meetings when they have ideas or suggestions to share. In response, you should ask questions that highlight the reasons you believe that idea or suggestion to be unsound or unworkable. Keep your response collegiate and moderated. If your questions are good and well worded, you should be able to make your point. Here again, your professional skills, social acumen and courtesy will come into play and can result in increased professional credibility, as well as elevate you in the eyes of your peers and the client.

To do anything else would be just ridiculous!

The Social Impact of a Consulting Career

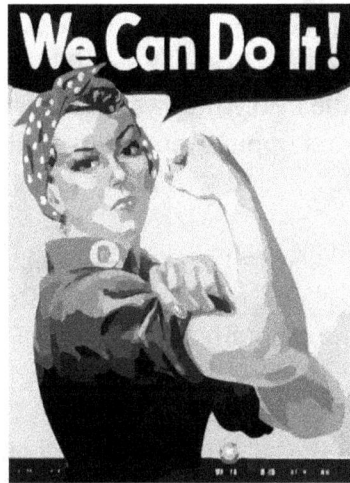

One of the most important reasons we work is to make a living and the living standard we establish is usually determined by how much money we make. A career in technology consulting can provide a better than average wage for those hardy souls willing and able to withstand the rigors of constant travel, new faces, new places, living out of a suitcase, always eating, sleeping and working in unfamiliar surroundings……. and all of this is done…… alone. If these working conditions seem a bit extreme then you might be a better fit in a local corporate IT department.

If you are married or in a seriously committed relationship your spouse or significant will pay a price for your career choice, as well. As will your children, your pets and the rest of your extended family. Technology consulting can pay well but sometimes money is an unequal substitute for missing your child's soccer tournament, spelling bee or dance recital, your anniversary or your dad's hip replacement surgery.

Things you used to fix or maintain around the house may have to wait for you to either take vacation or hire a handyman…..

unless, of course, your spouse or significant is handy and has the time. Remember, your spouse will be making the majority of the home related decisions in your absence and will have to handle everything you both used to do: kids, house, cars, yard, pets, shopping, cooking, laundry (not to mention a fulltime job).......and will likely be a little lonely, too.

Stable, creative couples can make this work if each understands and accepts the adjustments required. Throw in a gigantic amount of faith and trust while you are at it.

Most technology consultants travel about 10 months out of each year.....amounting to thousands of air miles and hundreds of hours spent in airports, buses and taxis just getting to and from the client site. Factor in unfamiliar weather, meals eaten alone and time spent in ever-changing hotels looking for the perfect pillow. Consulting contracts often include provisions for a consultant to commute home every weekend. However, the weekend won't be like it was when the consultant worked closer to home. Friday will be a travel day, as will Sunday evening or if you are lucky, an 'O'dark:30' flight out on Monday morning from which you will go directly to work. You will learn to sleep on airplanes and love peanuts in tiny packages.

As in any work setting, consultants will interact with other consultants and client employees during the workday on a professional basis then sometimes join them later at after-hour social events. Details of personal lives will likely be shared and friendships will be formed. Some of these associations may result in future consulting work. Guard against becoming too familiar with client employees lest the client form the opinion that you are more interested in socialization than in your role as a consultant on the client's project. You are being paid to guide the client employees in installing or upgrading a vital system not the drum major for office antics.

The development of romantic relationships at the client site for married consultant is obviously a very bad idea. Such relationships are also perilous for the unmarried consultant. Not only will your moral standards be called into question by the client, there is an increased likelihood such trysts will distract from, interrupt and delay the project......not to mention what could happen if one participant reacts badly to a breakup. Integrity never sleeps and never takes a holiday.

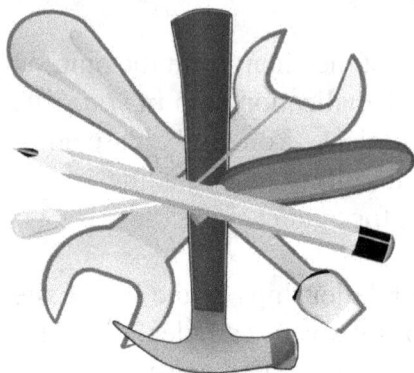

Tools of the Trade

When you call a plumber, you don't ask him if he knows how to use a pipe wrench. You just expect that he does because that tool is such an essential part of his work.

Consultants also have essential tools that are sometimes taken for granted. Tool #1 is a computer and if a person answers to the title of technology consultant that person should know his/her way around a computer keyboard. Some of the consultant's tools lie deep within the 'glowing blue screen.' For instance, within the Microsoft Office suite lurk Access, Excel, Outlook, PowerPoint, Project, Visio and Word......and Squiggles. All await your command.

Consultants routinely send documents prepared with these tools or with similar tools to clients. A responsible consultant uses every tool in their arsenal to ensure that these documents bear a professional message and a polished appearance..... these documents are representing that consultant, and the consultant's company.

A feature in Word, and similar word processing packages, allows the consultant to collaborate with peers and with management before finalizing a collaborative document. These packages allow consultants to track potential changes and to add notes. That is a very useful feature and helps ensure qual-

Don Wynn

ity and accuracy in the finalized communication. Consultants have to remember to apply the 'accept/reject changes' feature before sending documents to clients or that client will be reading your rough draft instead of the finished copy.

The 'spell/grammar' check feature is indispensable; especially for those who are phonics challenged. And for those who got an 'A' on the unit on sentence diagramming in 4th grade, you are not so outstanding at English grammar; sentence structure, capitalization and punctuation that you can afford to overlook this handy tool. This feature allows the consultant to easily see where a document may have violated some rule of good writing. The program typically puts little squiggly lines under words or phrases in the text where something is questionable. The program isn't always right so the author is expected to review each potential problem and to accept it as it is or to make appropriate changes. In addition, words and abbreviations associated with your work can easily be added to the dictionary to prevent them from causing edit errors in the future.

A problem occurs when consultants casually review documents and send the document despite the squiggles. When that document or e-mail is distributed those squiggly lines may still be visible and the client receives an e-mail or document that has editing marks throughout. This sends a message that if the consultant sends sloppy, incomplete communications that consultant will possibly be sloppy and negligent in his/her other work for the client. The client will not notice if documents don't have squiggly lines but they certainly will if they do have them. Details, details, the devil is in the details. It is the consultant's job is to pay attention to details. This type of detail may equate to a minor distraction but professional consultants don't want anything to have a negative impact regardless of the size of the impact. That document represents you, don't go half dressed.

These features may seem like the 'Easy' button but it cannot replace thorough editing by the author. Sometimes, the editing software does not mark an error if the error doesn't fail some standard test. For instance, if you meant to say something did not happen but inadvertently typed that word twice….the meaning conveyed is that it did happen. In other words, the consultant should also read and re-read for context, composition and clarity before transmitting. The automated 'Easy' button cannot replace the human factor for final review. The author is responsible for polishing their work.

Consultants must use all the tools that are available to them while understanding that even the finest, most modern and technologically advanced tools have limitations. A professional consultant produces a professional quality product when writing code, designing a program interface or writing his family's holiday greeting letter and should use similar attention to detail in all written communications. The quality and appearance of professional work is the responsibility of the professional consultant.

On second thought, these Squiggles may be the same monsters that used to live under my bed when I was a child. They may have simply moved into editing software by day and live under the bed at night. I'll need different tool tonight, a flashlight!

Uh Oh
Oops
Dang It!

E-mail provides plenty of opportunities for people to make
mistakes. These mistakes are
easy to make but they are also
easy to avoid if you just take a
few extra seconds before hitting
the 'send' button.

It is easy to attach documents to an e-mail without 'accepting
changes' when the document was created with 'track changes'
on. It is embarrassing when this gets inadvertently dissemi-
nated internally but can be far more damaging when that incomplete document is sent outside of your company. It makes
your company look silly and the sender look sloppy and unprofessional.

'Reply all' is another e-mail capability that can lead to problems if improperly used. Sometimes, the consultant may get
an e-mail message that is addressed to everyone in the company but that e-mail might requests only from specific recipients. For example, an e-mail may ask 22 company consultants
to provide serial numbers from their laptops or other computer
equipment along with specified details. If each respondent
sent their specific information to every other respondent.....
well, you do the math. The sender should be careful to avoid
the 'reply all' feature unless the circumstances really warrant

a broad reply. A 'broadcast' reply will cause each recipient to spend valuable time reviewing e-mail not meant for them. Most e-mail systems process a lot of mail and 'broadcast' replies add an unnecessary burden on the system and jam inboxes needlessly.

'Reply all' can also be damaging if the recipient actually wanted to respond only to the sender or to select recipients. The sender may have added notes that are not appropriate for everyone on the original distribution list. A good rule of thumb to follow is to avoid putting anything in an e-mail that could not be distributed widely.

'Forwarding' e-mail comes with its own set of problems, especially if the original e-mail is lengthy and not pertinent to the current reply. 'Forward' sends the entire e-mail stream and not just the most current message.

'Flaming' e-mail sometimes happens when people respond too quickly to a note that appears to attack or to be negative toward the recipient. Emotion is important because it adds to the passion that consultants should have but it is important to squeeze negative emotions out of e-mail and other communications channels.

Consultants should train themselves to ask a few questions just before they hit the 'send' button.

Is this e-mail addressed to the appropriate people?

If using the 'Reply All' feature, should everyone on the address line get this message?

If a message is being forwarded, does the recipient need to see all the previous messages in the stream?

Is the message clear and without combative language?

Am I responding appropriately to the issue I am addressing?

Is there any of the other communications option better suited to this message?

Have I thoroughly reviewed this e-mail so I come across as literate?

Exercising a little more care before sending a message will help consultants make the point they intend to make. Exercising the appropriate care will make communications more effective and will reduce confusion.

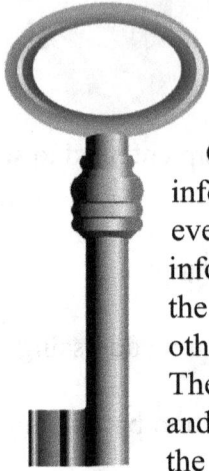

Key Words

Google has become an essential tool in the information age. Almost everyone who has ever used a computer has used Google to find information, get directions or search articles on the internet. A major component of Google and other search tools is the use of 'Key Words'. These words speed our searches for information and make it very easy for people to hone in on the specific information that is needed.

Consultants are aware of the importance of key words in their resumes. They are especially aware of key words that are likely to be used by prospective clients when they perform searches. Resumes are crafted with a consideration of key words in mind.

Consultants should also be aware of another type of key word. This type of key word plays a part in every communications channel. These words are key because they tend to have more impact than other words, sometimes positive and sometimes negative. It is important for consultants to realize which words generally fall into each category so that the positive words can be stressed and used more often and the negative words can be downplayed and used less often. Of course, there are no absolutes because context plays a significant role in effective communications.

For example, the word 'I' is an assertive word when stating an opinion. Consultants are often asked for professional opinions because providing opinions and guidance is a large part of the work of a consultant. When providing an opinion, using 'I' implies responsibility and accountability. It is unequivocal. When communicating with someone in this context, 'I' is a clear word.

When discussing the work of a group of collaborators, the word 'I' conveys an entirely different meaning. It sends a message to the other members of the team that undermines team dynamics. The 'I' word may be a subtle message but the team will hear it loud and clear. In the context of team activities, the word 'We' is much more positive and constructive. It recognizes the contribution of the entire team and fosters a sense of team and increases team dynamics.

The converse can also be true, using 'We' when discussing work that is clearly not the result of team collaboration can be negative because it can appear that the person using it is uncertain and that they don't want to be held accountable alone. They seem to be preparing to share responsibility and accountability if things don't go as planned. That is another subtle message that is heard loud and clear by the group.

Even when a single consultant has primary responsibility for a specified task, it is not uncommon for that consultant to have collaborated with colleagues within the team. When reporting results in this context, it is appropriate to use 'I' but it is also appropriate to say, "I had help from Joe Smith on this." In that context, you let the client know that they are getting the benefit of the experience and knowledge of other resources within the project team or from within the company. The consultant acknowledges the contributions that other people have made to his/her work without passing responsibility for its outcome to them.

There are no absolute rules that can be applied as to the appropriate words to use in every set of circumstances but it is important to realize that the words used can help the client develop an opinion of individual consultants and by extension, of your company as a whole.

Through Rain,
Through Sleet,
Through the Dark of Night

E-mail (almost) always gets through but is it always the best channel to use when a consultant needs to communicate with someone? Of course, the answer is a resounding, 'NO'. Consultants have a wide variety of options available but sometimes seem to choose e-mail as though it is ideal in every situation.

E-mail takes time to prepare and can clog the 'in box' of recipients. Using e-mail can actually increase the workload for people who are already busy. E-mail sometimes develops an 'afterlife' when circulated well beyond the expectations of the sender. Some even become 'spaghetti e-mails' where a single e-mail message initiates seemingly endless numbers of responses that become part of the e-mail string.

By its very nature, e-mail imparts a sense that the message is both urgent and important. Despite careful preparation, covering complex topics or sensitive issues via email can be tricky. Assess the appropriateness and complexity of the topic when determining to use e-mail over another form of communication. Ask yourself, if the immediacy of e-mail is important enough to risk possible confusion or misinterpretation.

An e-mail should be short and to-the-point without being blunt, seemingly argumentative, demeaning or accusatory. Brevity can prove difficult when the topic is complex. If an e-mail message is misinterpreted by the reader it may elicit an equally curt reply when no offense to the initial recipient was intended. Hurt feelings or damaged egos consume valuable time and energy to repair.

Why don't consultants simply make a phone call? This option is quick and easy and it has the added benefit of immediacy while assuring accuracy. By choosing a phone call, the caller can gauge the response in the voice of the recipient, and a phone conversation is more personal and lends more privacy to sensitive issues. Person-to-person communication also allows the caller to explain the message in the detail required and allows the respondent to answer questions and clarify confusing points immediately, especially if the topic is lengthy and complex.

If a consultant cannot reach the person by telephone, voice mail allows the consultant to leave a short message. A reasonable definition of 'short message' is 10 seconds! Your definition may be longer than 10 seconds but it should never reach the 2-minute mark.

If several people need to be contacted at once, the consultant should schedule a quick conference call or face-to-face meeting. Good conference calling equipment is usually available and consultants typically work in facilities where conference rooms are available. The benefit of conference calls and meet-

Don Wynn

ings is that everyone can provide input to the entire group at once. Questions can be asked and points can be clarified. Everyone should leave with a better understanding of the issues. Speakerphones can be problematic because so much depends upon the equipment and on the acoustics of the room.

Text messaging is a great option for short messages. This allows consultants to get important information to people who may be in meetings, or otherwise unable to speak with the caller. The recipient can see the message without disrupting the meeting. If a consultant cannot get into a conference call for some reason, it is possible to communicate the problem to the meeting organizer in this convenient way. The definition of 'short message' here is one or two lines. Avoid trying to convey complex messages this way because text messages require more effort to read and, like e-mail, can be misinterpreted and cause unintended confusion if used inappropriately.

Any communication a consultant makes should reflect their core values of professionalism. And remember, e-mail and text messages are (potentially) stored forever.

Your Words Go Here

for everyone to see

The Billboard on the Hill

Imagine for a second that there is a billboard on the hill in front of your house. There is another just like it in front of your church, in front of the office of your company, in front of your children's school, in front of the client's office and home and in front of co-worker's homes. Imagine that these special billboards are everywhere.

These billboards are reserved for your own personal use. They are multi-media. You can put text on them but you can also put pictures, cartoons, short movies, as well as sound and even music. You can display your creativity and put things on your billboard that entertain people and may even make them smile. You can take a position on things that are in the news. You can comment on the events of the day. You can record your life and opinions for posterity.

These billboards have become so popular that more and more people have them. They can be fun and entertaining. Some are insightful and thought provoking some are even informative. They can also be wrong and hurtful. Billboards can damage relationships and can potentially destroy them.

The familiar school-yard chant, 'sticks and stones can break my bones but words will never hurt me!' is wrong. Words can be very painful and that has been proven to be true many times

80   Don Wynn

over as society has entered the information age.

The phenomenon of personal billboards has one critical flaw that has not yet been resolved. The flaw is that information displayed on a billboard is a virtually a permanent message. The billboard owner cannot erase the content once something has been displayed. After the content is initially displayed, it may be included in other billboards that are owned by other people. That is, erasing the first billboard may not remove the message from the community. Even though the sentiment behind a particular message changes, the owner of the billboard cannot implement the change. There are no 'take it backs' or 'do overs' in billboard land!

Now imagine all the perfect people and organizations that you know. Be sure to include yourself in the pool of people being considered. If you believe you can think of even one person (other than young children) who is perfect, your relationship is probably based upon infatuation. Some irrational feeling blurs your perspective. People and organizations have flaws, this includes you. The people who understand (and usually overlook) a person's flaws are the people who are closest to them. My wife understands my flaws and she has the good grace to love me in spite of them.

The point is that perfect people don't exist and that you will forever be disappointed if you expect perfection in the people you work with. Finally, imagine the frustrations that you face everyday as you deal with imperfect people and with imperfect organizations. That frustration can harm you unless you can find a way to vent and relieve the psychic pressure that it causes. Just describing the stressful event or stressful person has a calming effect. You may think that the billboards that are available to you would be a good way to relieve the pressure.

Billboards simply are never a good way to resolve this type of stress……………..

Those billboards can make your frustration and psychic pressure even worse because they act in a very public way. Maybe, just maybe, you should consider other approaches rather than to put such sensitive information on billboards for everyone to see. Talk to your friends and co-workers, talk to your spouse, talk to you manager, and keep a paper journal. Do whatever you have to do but you should consider other options before resorting to your own personal billboard.

The passage of time, unforeseen clarifying factors and mitigating circumstances may serve to embarrass you and undermine your personal and professional credibility. Find a way to deal with imperfection without erecting a permanent billboard in front of your house or in front of the client's house.

Where Am I and
What Am I Doing?

Sometimes, I find myself asking this question as I walk away from the coffee pot after a casual conversation with a client employee. That is exactly the wrong time to be asking that. I should keep that in mind before having any casual conversations at all.

The 'Go Live' date (the culmination date of the project; the date when a transition is made to use the new system) is almost always a point of discussion on implementation projects. Looking back over my consulting career, I can't remember a single time when I felt that the client was as ready as I wanted them to be. It may be a characteristic of consultants to feel that they can be better prepared if given more time.

The responsibility for representing a consulting company and all of their technology consultants belongs to the Project Manager (PM) and the consulting company's management. The Project Management Team should listen to all the consultants' concerns and then should present a united front to the client. Take heed, it can be very unprofessional and divisive if individual consultants discuss their individual concerns or opinions outside of the appropriate forums.

Client employees are also frequently concerned about the project schedule and the 'Go Live' date. They may solicit the individual opinions of consultants about these topics. How should consultants respond when these questions come up in casual conversations? When those questions are asked, consultants should always ask themselves, "Where am I," "What am I doing here"? The answer is: that consultant is at a client site and is representing their consulting company as a professional employee. That should guide their interactions. An appropriate answer to the client's question could be, "There are a lot of things to be done and the team is working hard to meet the schedule." That should be the consultant's response even if they have concerns about the team's ability to meet the schedule.

When a consultant has schedule concerns, those concerns should be voiced to the Project Manager who may have more complete information as he/she receives input from the entire team. The PM serves as the sole contact point with the consulting team and with the client on this important issue.

Once a decision has been made, consultants should support that decision as strongly as possible. Individual consultants should not voice their individual concerns to the client unless the Project Manager is part of the discussion and has voiced support for that consultant's position and/or concern prior to meeting the client (no surprises, please).

This is not intended to stifle input but it will cause your company to present a unified front to the client on this important topic.

Going Native

Going Native does not mean dressing in native costumes and taking hula lessons while you are on vacation. It also does not mean that you act like Robinson Crusoe and live off the land, fish with spears, drink cocoa nut milk and lounge in a hammock in the tropical sun.

In the slang of technology consulting, it means developing a relationship with client employees that has a negative impact on your ability to meet your responsibilities to your company and to your client. When you go to a client site to work, you shouldn't have to be reminded about whom you actually work for!

Consultants are typically very personable people. They enjoy their work, enjoy their teammates and often develop close relationships with them. Consultants also enjoy the company of many client employees they work with. Working together with client employees through sometimes stressful situations often results in closer relationships between consultants and client employees. That seems only natural.

In fact, a consultant needs to have a strong collegial relationship with all of his/her teammates, which includes other consultants on the project, client management and client employees. The entire team needs to work together in a cohesive way to meet the goals of the project. Consultants want the client to recognize the professional contributions they make; and if the relationship between the consultant and the client is strong enough, the client may come directly to an individual consultant, project manager or consulting company manager when future projects are anticipated.

Consultants need their clients and former clients to promote them and their consulting companies to friends in industry. Consultant/client relations are vital because former clients frequently serve as reference accounts as consultants seek future business. All of this is based upon the professional contributions consultants have made to the project, or it should be.

Inappropriate relationships can damage your reputation and can damage relationships with the client. In spite of the fact that consultants need to develop close professional relationships with clients, they need to be aware that there is a line that should not be crossed. Consultants can never use a friendship as a justification to divulge sensitive information about a client, or about that consultant's employer. Consultants sometimes have discussions within the project consulting team at the client site where they discuss different options that could impact the project. The details of those conversations should remain confidential within the consulting team. Your project manager will convey the 'consulting company's recommendations' to the client. Someone who has 'gone native' could damage your company's relationship with the client by providing them with details about your company's internal discussions.

Regardless of how an individual consultant may feel about it, there is an invisible line that separates them from the employees of the client. Consultants are the experts that client employees look to for support, for guidance and for help. There is a natural distinction between consultants and the client. As hard as it may be at times, consultants must recognize that distinction and must maintain it. Consultants are not simply co-workers with client employees. Consultants are at the client site in a professional capacity and need to always be aware of that.

Developing close relationships may be difficult to avoid, this is especially true when projects are to relatively long term in nature. Consultants sometimes work shoulder to shoulder in some pretty stressful situations with client employees. Under those conditions, it may be somewhat natural to develop some close relationships because a consultant may work at the same client site several times over a period of years. Consultants need to be aware of the negative impacts that 'going native' can have on their work and on the relationship that your company has with the client organization.

All of these relationships add a dimension to life but are they all appropriate? Think about it! Would it be appropriate if consultants allowed a relationship with client employees to affect their professional activities or professional judgment? Would it be appropriate if sensitive information was divulged to a client employee at lunch or over drinks in the evening? Would it be appropriate if a client employee was told the details of internal discussions that consultants have within the consulting team at the site?

The answer to a resounding, NO!

Dorm Rules

Can you remember those days in the dorm where a grad student lived in the first room down the hall and was responsible for enforcing the rules? You may recall, 'turn that music down', 'no cooking allowed', and 'get rid of that space heater', and on and on. Consultants don't live in dorms anymore but they do work in spaces that have a lot in common with dorms. Their workspaces are usually cramped and may be shared with several others. Things that happen in these spaces affect everyone!

One big difference between professional workspace and dorm rooms is that workspace doesn't have that grad student to enforce the rules. The basic tenets of good manners, courtesy and common sense are largely unwritten but are no less important than those which have been codified. Everything that happens within a shared space has some impact on every other person within that space.

Noise is a big concern. Consultants should remember that they are in a professional office. In the words of Miss Ruth, my granddaughter's kindergarten teacher, consultants should remember to use their 'indoor voices'. Limit extraneous conversation as much as possible, constant chatter can be as distracting as loud noises. If a conversation needs to extend for more than a few minutes, look for a vacant conference room. Some people may prefer to have background music while they work but everyone's taste in music may not be the same. A good set of earphones can prevent your music from bothering others while keeping in mind that it may not always be appropriate to listen to music at a client site even if you use earphones!

Noises and odors associated with eating at your desk can also be unwelcome by your neighbors. Some people simply make a lot of noise when they eat; they rattle utensils, plastic food containers and bags. If someone kept a bag of Doritos in their drawer and snacked on them all day, the crinkly bag could become an irritant just like the proverbial 'dripping faucet.'

Eating at the desk may be convenient for people when deadlines are looming but it can also cause a distraction for people in the area. The smells alone can become an issue and can linger well into the afternoon, especially if the food containers are discarded in the wastebaskets in the office. Over time, that practice can attract insects adding another dimension to that particular problem.

Phone usage can be another problem. The older members of my family used to yell into the phone but then they used crank-type phones that lacked volume control. New fangled electronics have made yelling unnecessary. Miss Ruth would say, "Use your phone voice, please," which is even lower than your 'indoor voice'. Since almost everyone has a cell phone, it is easy to move to an area where fewer people will be bothered if an extended phone call is made, and especially if that call is not work related.

Fans and heaters can be a divisive issue, as well. The comfort level of everyone may be affected by any change to the temperature of the room.

We should all live by Miss Ruth's advice and 'Be a good neighbor!'

Don Wynn

Casual Fridays

In the olden days, Casual Friday meant that men could wear an open collar shirt without a tie. Women could wear a matching pantsuit with flats. Most people really appreciated the change on Fridays to let their hair down a little. Everyone seemed more comfortable.

A lot has changed since the inception of Casual Fridays. In fact, the employees at some companies now dress casually all the time. The meaning of what is 'casual' has also changed dramatically over time.

In the past, 'Casual Friday' attire meant what we now refer to as 'Business Casual' and wasn't much of a step down from outright formal clothing (for men a suit, button-down shirt with tie; for women a tailored dress with high heels). Shined shoes were always a must, no matter what day it was, as was a neat haircut or neatly coifed hairdo. Casual attire was reserved for your backyard barbeques or attendance at youth sporting events. The phrase 'Business Casual' is still in use but people seem to consider 'Casual Attire' and 'Business Casual' to be the same thing. They are definitely not the same!

Since the inception of 'Casual Fridays', people began to embrace more casual look all of the time. Some people began wearing exercise clothes almost everywhere they might go. It is difficult to determine if that person is headed to the gym, on the way home from the gym, headed to work or to the mall.

Somehow it even became acceptable to wear sweat shirts, sweat pants and flip flops to work.

That was bad enough but when the 'grunge' look became popular because people intentionally began wearing torn clothing. At first, the tears were on the knees and upper thighs. Then the tears began showing up in places where there should not be any tears. A lot of people adopted the 'grunge' look in an f to look edgy and hip; they even called it 'shabby chic'. Besides torn clothing, men started going to work sporting yesterday's stubble and women began wearing all manner of lingerie and other sheer, clingy outerwear to the office.

How does this cultural transition affect consultants and consulting? Consultants should keep in mind to use the traditional meaning of 'Business Casual' when in a casual situation at the client site. Always wear clean, well-maintained clothes that are neat in appearance. Avoid the wrinkled, unkempt, unshaven look; leave that for your personal time. Consultants have personal freedom to be themselves just like everyone has but they also must exercise good judgment when deciding the appropriateness of a particular 'look'. When a consultant adheres to the traditional 'Business Casual' dress on casual days at client sites, they project a more professional image of themselves and of their companies.

"Business Casual' usually means a business shirt open at the collar, dress slacks, no jacket and no tie. A slight departure from this attire is 'Resort Casual' for out-of-the-office occasions held at a resort type location. 'Resort Casual' means a polo type shirt or other neatly pressed shirt (Hawaiian shirts are my favorite), neatly pressed pants or even a pair of walking shorts, as appropriate for the meeting location and theme. Sandals or athletic shoes still trump flip flops but no matter what shoes you choose make sure they are clean and in good repair. Gentlemen, a well maintained haircut never goes out of style. Ladies, when in a professional setting consider a hairstyle which does not require you to continuously swipe away tendrils of hair from in front of your face, such movements can detract from an otherwise polished and professional appearance.

These are just a few pointers to help you present yourself in the most professional light. Look the part, act the part. However, do not let 'political correctness' interfere with good sense when it comes to health related issues. When your feet hurt you hurt all over. Comfortable shoes can make the difference between a successful day at work and a dreadful day at work. I wore clogs to work for a period of time while experiencing a painful foot ailment but returned to more professional looking footwear when the problem cleared up.

I won't be wearing my clogs (unless necessary), torn jeans (never) or my beloved Hawaiian shirts to work. All bets are off when I am working from my home office where the definition of casual is c-a-s-u-a-l. (We won't go there in this Soft Skill Tip).

Private Conversations
.............in Public Places

Consultants, as a group, spend quite a bit of time in public places, in airplanes and airports, in buses and cabs, in hotel lobbies, in restaurants and sometimes in bars. Life in public places is just one of the side effects of the career in consulting. After a while, it is easy to become desensitized to the fact that so much time is spent in these public places. Privacy is lost but consultants don't seem to notice!

We readily notice when some total stranger or group of strangers has a private conversation in a public place. Everyone around them can hear. For some reason, we may not recognize it when we do that! Loud conversations in public places are rude but they can also violate the trust that clients place in their consultants. Consulting can be sensitive work because it involves sensitive details about the operations of client organizations. Consultants know the details of their client's business practices, the good and the bad details. Consultants know financial details and usually know when and where the client may be wasting money. Consultants have the experience, training and access to know some of their client's business details even better than most employees of the client know them.

As professionals, consultants have an obligation to protect and

94 Don Wynn

safeguard the business details of clients. For that reason, always be conscious of surroundings when in face-to-face conversations and on cell phone calls. Consultants should always remember the mantra, 'mind your tongue because you never know who is listening.' It is also a good idea to maintain a 'zipped lip' after leaving a client's project because prospective clients may get the idea you will talk about them when you leave their project. The watchword is 'confidentiality'.

Consultants should try to avoid having private conversations in public places. However, the demands of consulting work often dictate that business be conducted on cell phones and, at times, in public places. A few, simple guidelines to consider might be appropriate. For example, it would be a good idea to avoid audibly mentioning the client's name in these conversations. Recognize that people near the client location might know the consultants on the project and may be aware of the work that the consultant does. Consultants meet so many people that they may not remember the people at the next table in a restaurant even though those people recognize the consultant. Consultants are the experts who are at the client site to resolve serious problems or to do other complex work. They may not rock stars but people in the area of the client site may still recognize them. Be conscious of surroundings and move to more isolated places when there is a need to have private conversations.

If someone overhears a conversation that seems to reveal private information about the client, regardless of whether that information is good or bad, the consultant has violated one of the most basic tenets of a responsible professional.

Let's talk about Social Issues

Let's just face it; there are some topics that can be very divisive and polarizing. They can disturb the harmony, undermine unity, and call in question a consultant's professionalism. Almost everyone has some very strong opinions about specific issues and/or events and beliefs they hold dear. There will never be common consensus regarding such issues as the death penalty, women's reproductive options, gun control, gay marriage or racial issues, and the list goes on and on.

As a society, it may be very important to discuss these issues even if consensus is unlikely. In the over-all sense, discussion can be a very good thing. That is especially true if everyone in the discussion can maintain civility and if they really listen to and appreciate the input and position of all the people who are participating in the discussion. Unfortunately, such conversations often lead to heated debate which succeeds in convincing no one and inflaming everyone.

If someone enters into a conversation with the best of intentions, it could still go in directions that were never expected or intended. People can become insulted or can inadvertently insult others without meaning to. The person issuing the insult might not even know that they had done it. A consultant can alienate a client and/or client employees without knowing it and that alienation could make it difficult, if not impossible, for that consultant to do the work they are there to do.

Don Wynn

So then, what should a consultant do? Making a conscious decision to avoid having extended or in-depth conversations about controversial topics is very sound idea. Even flippant remarks in passing about such topics rarely lead to a positive result. In fact, engaging in long conversations during work hours, no matter how benign the topic, can give the impression that the consultant has time to waste and sees no urgency related to the project schedule.

Conversations concerning topics other than the work at hand are inevitable. Try to keep your comments brief, polite and neutral in nature. For example, if the conversation is about the death penalty and someone says, "The death penalty is a terrible thing." The consultant can respond with something like, "Our country has had to make some very difficult decisions." Almost everyone would agree with that and the consultant will have avoided taking a particular stand. These comments do not provide a clear idea of the consultant's personal position or opinion on that topic. People might be able to agree that the death penalty is a difficult decision, regardless of their support for or lack of support of the death penalty.

It is still inappropriate to have such discussions while at lunch or while participating in a dinner outing with the client and/or client employees. Team events are often pretty informal affairs and can give the impression that the team is simply a group of friends enjoying an evening out. Consultants should understand those are business events that are just being held away from the office and should act accordingly.

Consultants are active and engaged people and may have

strongly held opinions about a variety of 'hot button' topics and may feel compelled to share their opinions with people they encounter. Consultants who feel that compulsion should reconsider engaging in such conversations at work and work-related events. Work relationships can be irreparably damaged following discussion of such polarizing topics. No one will be persuaded to change their respective opinion(s) so......keep a lid on it.

Don't Be Blue

When you seem a little sad to someone who is close to you, they might say, "Don't be blue," and may try to cheer you up. When a teammate seems a bit down it is always nice to give them a little extra support and encouragement. It is also pretty nice to get that support when you need it yourself. Unfortunately, the topic of this Soft Skill Tip is not that type of 'blue.'

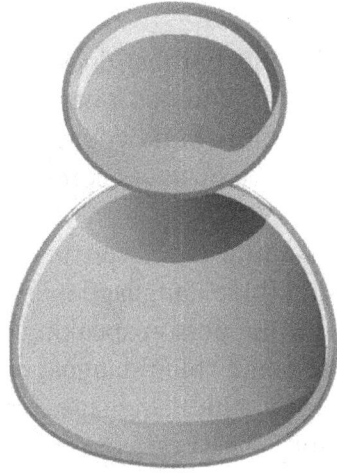

This 'blue' refers to language that might not be appropriate in a professional setting. That language might fit in a locker room or a pool hall but it doesn't cast you as a professional or the company you represent in a positive light. In fact, it can make you look crude and ill- mannered, and diminish you in the eyes of your clients. 'Blue' language can be very offensive to some people and can definitely change their perception of you if they hear you using 'blue' language. At the very least, the use of crude language will cast doubt on the size of your vocabulary so don't be surprised if some anonymous donor places a Thesaurus on your desk.

As a seasoned technology consultant you instinctively know the words that you should avoid when representing your company so I won't identify them directly. Generally, these words have 4 letters and their usage is frowned upon in most business settings. You see them in comedy routines and in movies and songs but that doesn't make them acceptable in business settings. You don't necessarily want 'street cred'. You actually want to build your professional credentials and reputation within the business community.

Consulting work can be characterized as stressful at times. Using 'blue' language might be excused if its use is infrequent and if the person speaking is under pressure. People may excuse some 'blue' language during obvious times of stress as long as 'blue' language is not a constant part of any conversation. The best course is to never use 'blue' language even when under stress!

Maybe a good rule of thumb to use when deciding what is appropriate would be to use words that you could use in front of your mother without fear of embarrassing her or of feeling the wraith of parental punishment. Use the same words and demeanor that you might use if you were making an address to a PTA meeting or to the Boy Scouts.

You want to make people smile at your professional demeanor rather than to cringe at your language!

Island Time

Travel, travel, travel… technology consulting typically involves a lot of travel. Some consultants travel in their work 100% of the time. In other words, they are away from their homes and home cities every day they work. Even with all of that travel, consultants are not tourists and are not on vacation. If consultants are not conscious of the image that they project to clients, the impression can be given that they are tourists. Technology consultants should consciously avoid giving the impression that you are primarily at the client site to enjoy the scenery and take in the local color.

Avoid the use of slang phrases that someone might use when they are on a leisure trip. For example, if you are on vacation to an island in the Caribbean Ocean, you may go to breakfast late and might make a reference to 'island time' to explain your casual schedule. A tourist might say that they were 'hanging out' at the café for lunch. Consultants should avoid making any comment like that to anyone at the client site. The client could easily associate those phrases and others like them with vacations. They could form an opinion that the consultant will take a casual approach to the project or to their tasks at the client site.

Just because you, as a consultant are on time every day does not give you the right to comment on the timeliness of others. If a client employee is late for a meeting, it would be easy to make some slang comment about their tardiness. If Joe is late, it might be tempting to say something like, "Joe's on Joe Time," or "He's in Joe World." Comments like that may not be intended to insult or to voice an opinion of Joe but they could foster a negative image anyway. You are responsible for making sure you are on time every time, and the responsibility of the client management to ensure that their employees are also on time. Comments from you are unwelcome and can portray you as a verbal prankster whose intent is to self-promote by diminishing the actions of others.

The best approach is to leave side comments and vacation slang on the beach when you head for the client site.

Don Wynn

What Do I Owe?

Relationships usually provide benefits to the people in those relationships while imposing responsibilities on those in the relationships. Almost everyone participates in a variety of relationships ranging from immediate families to extended families, to their employer, co-workers, communities, professional associates, religious institutions, political parties, social clubs, etc. The point is that most people lead active lives and are involved in a variety of relationships at some level. When responsibilities to one relationship conflict with the responsibilities of other relationships, an evaluation is required and choices have to be made.

People usually enter into new relationships with the expectation of some benefit for participation. Their initial focus may be, "What's in it for me"? Over time, they may realize that their relationships exact a 'price' in terms of responsibilities in turn for the expected benefits. That 'price' should be welcomed and must be acted upon if the benefits are to be enjoyed. If these responsibilities to your relationships are not met, then those relationships will certainly fail over time.

When I think about my relationships, I try to think in terms of, "What do I owe in return"? The answer to that question is very personal. Each of us has to develop an answer that fits us as individuals. You have to act upon your responsibilities and you cannot simply adopt the answers that another person has incorporated into his/her life.

When I think of family, I have a few simple responsibilities. I owe material and emotional support on a 24-7 basis whether in residence at home, as well as when I am traveling away from home. I want to do my part. Constant travel in my work makes this a tricky proposition that continually demands creative solutions to maintain the balance of work and home. I try to be present at every important event in the lives of my family, at graduations, weddings, birthdays and family reunions, etc. I should be there when it counts, but also realize that it is possible to miss events occasionally without failing in my responsibilities to my family.

When I think of co-workers, I have a few simple responsibilities. I owe consideration, support and honesty. I should respond as quickly as I can when help is needed. I also owe my co-workers a request for help when I need it. Sometimes the hardest responsibility to meet is the responsibility to depend upon co-workers for help. It is much easier to provide help than it is to ask for or to receive it gracefully. I have a responsibility to expect as much from my co-workers as I expect from myself…but I do not have a right to expect more. I have the responsibility to acknowledge the efforts and contributions of others. I have a responsibility to shoulder my part of the workload and to share the burden when I need help or when help is needed from me. I have a responsibility to hold my co-workers and myself accountable for the work that we do. I have a responsibility to accept responsibility for the results of my work.

Don Wynn

This is true when things go as planned, as well as when things seem to be going 'south' in a hurry.

When I think of clients, I have a few simple responsibilities. I have a responsibility to apply my professional knowledge and skill to the tasks that are assigned to me. I have a responsibility to act in a professional manner, to provide professional input and to accept the decisions of the client once they have heard my input. I have a responsibility to the team to act the way that cohesive, respectful team members should act. I have a responsibility to avoid becoming a divisive element. I have a responsibility to support long term project activities even if it means that I occasionally give up some family time and some weekends. Unfortunately, that responsibility may sometimes cause me to work a few holidays. There must be a balance here because the consultant cannot be expected to forgo every weekend and every holiday, or expect to never to work a weekend or a holiday.

When I think of my company, I have a few simple responsibilities. I have a responsibility to remember that I act as a representative of the company in all of my company related activities. My actions reflect on me as an individual but they also reflect on my company and on the other fine people who work here. I have a responsibility to provide honest work and to consider the impact of my actions on the company. I have a responsibility to communicate honestly and directly with management. This responsibility is even stronger when it relates to something I may take issue with. My responsibility does not stop when the subject is not positive. I have a responsibility to consider the needs of the company and to sometimes go beyond the basic requirements of my job.

Every relationship in life demands that you meet your responsibilities in that relationship if it is to be successful. Think about your relationships and make conscious decisions about them. If you want to be successful as a consultant you should think about the level of responsibility that a career in this profession entails and the impact it will have on all the other responsibilities you have.

Life in general and your relationships in particular, are about balance as much as anything else. Balance, it is all about balance.

Passion is More
Than Just a Fruit

Passion should be an ingredient in everything you do as a technology consultant. It is a cornerstone component of a top consultant and it is one of the things that separate them from all the other consultants in the industry. Consultants convey their passion to clients in many different ways. After working with a top consultant for a while, clients begin to expect to see passion in the work of the consultant because it is always there. Passion is an intangible but it should always be a part of the consulting environment.

Passion is hard to describe but everyone knows when it is present. Clients and fellow technology consultants know it too. Showing passion does not require a person to be loud and outgoing because it can be shown by people with all different personalities. Clients can tell when someone has passion when they hear conviction in the consultant's speech and when they can see passion in the consultant's eyes.

Passion conveys strong feelings and tells the client that the consultant cares about their work. The best technology consultants care about the products they work with, they care about their fellow technology consultants and about their company. They care about quality in their work. They care about details and don't leave things to chance. They care about their professional knowledge and practical education. They care about the contribution they make and you demand a lot from themselves. Passion conveys a sense of dedication to quality. Passion and all of the things that passion implies are some of the reasons that the projects of top consultants are successful. It is also one of the reasons that They can succeed in projects when other consultants and other consulting companies can't.

Passion may be even more important when communicating with prospective clients in phone calls, at conferences and presentations. It is a strong differentiator when prospective clients are making decisions about their consulting partners. Consultants need to give prospective clients as many reasons as they can to help them select them for client projects.

Passion is contagious. Consistently showing passion helps build a team of people with similar traits. Passionate people are drawn to the team and to the project and synergy develops.

The best consultants are conscious of this important ingredient and nurture it. They help their fellow technology consultants develop and show their passion. Passion is at the heart of success.

Walking Around Sense

In the south, there is a phrase that describes something that all technology
consultants need. It describes a trait that
is fundamental to success. Consultants
need to be able to think on their feet, in
other words, to have a generous amount
of 'walking around sense'. They need to
quickly adapt their actions and responses
to the specific situations they face daily. Consultants sometimes have very little time to consider all of the options or
appropriate responses in a given situation. Engaging the brain
before engaging the mouth is a good place to start.

When consultants are interacting with someone at a client site
it is important to use their 'walking around sense.' 'Walking around sense' amounts to common sense applied quickly.
Consultants should remember where they are at all times and
with whom they are interacting and realize that the things consultants say or do can be taken out of context. A client company employee could 'edit' the consultant's words or actions into
a 'sound bite' for the purpose of advancing their own agenda.
Keep in mind that not all client employees are overjoyed that
outside consultants have been hired to make changes to the
client company's status quo and/or to their current operating
system.

Consultants should not be afraid to interact with client employees but they must use some 'walking around sense' to guide

their words and actions to avoid occasionally 'stepping in it'. By considering these possibilities in advance and establishing some guidelines, a consultant may be able to avoid making statements or sharing opinions that could lead to confusion or misinterpretation in the workplace. A state of confusion created by a misstep of a consultant will reflect badly on the consultant and the consulting company he/she represents long before it, if ever, reflects on the abilities, actions or cooperative efforts of client company employees. Consulting company policy cannot cover every possible situation and consultants cannot predict or anticipate every situation which might arise because the consulting environment is much too dynamic for that.

Don Wynn

Tobacco Anyone?

Tobacco usage is a personal choice
that consultants are certainly free to
make but they should be aware that
usage of those products could influence
the opinions that clients have about them. Tobacco usage
will impact personal hygiene unless the consultant takes
specific steps to counter that side effect. If the consultant frequently takes breaks in the work day to satisfy their tobacco
cravings, the client may see that as a waste of time.

There are many ways tobacco usage can affect the relationship between a consultant and clients and client employees.
For example, tobacco usage can have a dramatic effect on appearance and some colleagues may respond negatively to the
smell of tobacco products or may even have allergic reactions
to it. If a consultant cannot hold their tobacco dependence
in abeyance during working hours they should be especially
mindful of the impact that the side effects of tobacco usage
can have on their relationship with clients.

If you are a smoker, you are probably aware of the impact
that tobacco usage has on appearance and already pay close
attention to your personal and dental hygiene. A smoker's
breath can become stale, teeth are often discolored and smoke
always clings to their clothes and hair, thereby subjecting
co-workers to a less-than-aromatic work environment. Coun-
teracting this with generous amounts of cologne or breath

mints is not really helpful and may create additional issues for co-workers. Use of smokeless tobacco products can be equally distressing for non-smokers. This tobacco avenue may eliminate the smoke odor but creates a situation whereby the tobacco user must either 'spit or swallow.' Enough said about that!

Perhaps the most important impact could happen if a smoker continuously leaves the building or goes to the 'smoking court' for smoke breaks. Frequent breaks = reduced productivity, and may be perceived as client money being wasted. The client will form opinions about these breaks, especially if they are frequent and especially if they become extended.

The Political Season is Upon Us

We live in a country where everyone has the great privilege of participating in the selection of our political leaders. We are free to voice our individual opinions and debate the merits of issues and candidates as we view them. Sometimes our intent in such discourse is to convince others to adopt and support the aims and views we hold dear and our citizenship confers on us the right to vote to sustain those convictions and choices. Our democratic society thrives on active discussion of such topics.

There is a time and a place for almost everything. The client site is not the place to promote individual views and opinions. In this setting, a consultant's role is to provide representation of their company. The things consultants say and do can reflect on the entire company. In that context, a consultant's status as a private citizen becomes secondary, their opinions as private citizens become secondary, as well.

Consulting companies are generally not political organizations. They operate for-profit and need to be able to do business with a wide variety of client organizations. Consulting companies do not want the private opinions of their employees to influence their business relationship with clients. Every technology consultant should respect the need to separate private opinions from daily activities at client sites.

Consulting companies may fully support the rights of all

citizens to voice opinions and to participate as a supporter of political candidates, political parties and their associated platforms. The only requirement is that their consulting employees participate in those activities away from the client site and that their personal opinions are not construed as the opinion of the company.

Consultants should not openly support any political party or agenda while at the client site. Political badges, buttons or pins should not be worn even if the pin is small. Posters and placards should not be displayed in the workspace. Political screen savers should not be used. Consultants should not use the contact lists that they have developed through their work to send political messages, cartoons or jokes.

Consultants are free to enjoy their rights as citizens when they are away from the client and from the client site but should avoid bringing private matters into their professional arena.

Don Wynn

How to Make Incredibly Dull Presentations

Making a dull presentation is one of the easiest things to do. Most people can do it without even thinking about it. Just follow a few very simple rules and your presentations will be so dull that attendees will soon be asleep or, perhaps, slipping out the nearest exit.

The most important rule is to always speak in a monotone voice. Avoid changing the volume from one section of the speech to another. Loud, sudden noises or the rustling of papers may place emphasis on one point over others. It may also disturb the reverie of the audience. In fact, the best volume is low and soothing. For the most soothing effect, model your presentation after the lullabies your mother used to sing to you. Cadence should be slow, steady and predictable. Use the same pace, speed and volume throughout the presentation and you will be well on your way to presenting a truly forgettable speech.

Other rules relate to where you stand and how you move during the presentation. If possible, remain seated throughout the presentation. If the audience cannot see you, they can concentrate on your spoken message, drowsiness will result even faster. In those cases where you cannot avoid standing, you should stand rigidly behind the podium without making any unnecessary gestures with your hands or arms. Never under any circumstances, move away from the podium. Don't walk around in front of your audience, your movement provides a distraction and makes it difficult for them to take advantage of the opportunity to snooze. At this point, facial expressions and voice inflection are of no use.

Presentation materials can also be very distracting to the audience. Avoid using graphics or photographs especially ones that are in color. It is best to use text only and a small font, which requires strained concentration from the audience. The more text you use, the better. In fact, the dullest presenters will include every word in their presentation on their slides. They can then read the presentation in a steady, monotone voice for a 'double whammy' effect.

Never, under any circumstances, should you waiver from your prepared material. Don't engage in any dialog with the audience and don't make eye contact because that only encourages questions. If the audience really wants more detail or elaboration, they will do their research after getting home. If they ask questions, direct them to good reference material, if you happen to know any. Simply giving them the answer makes it too easy. People really appreciate what they have to work for!

If you really are feeling lively, you can keep a pocket full of loose change. At several points during your presentation, put your hand in your pocket and jiggle your change. The resulting sound should be just loud enough to really irritate your audience. But be aware the sound make may awaken the ones who are already asleep.

If you follow these simple rules, your audience will be commenting that your presentation was the dullest, biggest waste of time and most irritating presentation that they have ever attended as they rapidly exit the meeting hall. Their evaluation will most likely relieve you of any responsibility to shake hands or converse with any of your audience following the presentation. The people who were inclined to leave early will be thinking the same thing even if they don't take the time to tell you.

Snap, Crackle, Pop

I'll bet you thought this would somehow involve 3 elves and a bowl of cereal but it won't. It is about the sound that a cracking voice makes when you address an audience. That sound may go away quickly but it still leaves the audience with the impression that the speaker is uncomfortable, maybe even fearful of public speaking. The speaker is aware that their voice has cracked and that awareness can disrupt their chain of thought. A bumpy start can affect the entire presentation.

Since you want to make a positive impression on the audience and to exude professionalism, you want to eliminate that cracking sound when you begin to speak. Practicing a very simple exercise just before you begin to speak can help with that.

The trick is to acclimatize your vocal cords to the air temperature in the room before speaking. That cracking is caused because the speaker takes an initial deep breath immediately before they speak. That is a natural thing to do because the speaker wants to speak loud enough so the people at the back of the room can hear.

What you do in the minute or so immediately before you speak can help to control the cracking voice problem. The exercise is simple and effective. It will work without fail as long as you remember to do it. So what is this magic exercise for speakers? The exercise is to breathe through your mouth deeply several times before you speak. A nice rule of thumb is to start this exercise while you are being introduced. It only takes 2-3 good, deep breaths.

Some people do this automatically but others have to consciously make an effort to do it. If you are in the second group, make a mental note of this and remember to do it and you will reduce the risk of your voice cracking when you begin the presentation.

Of course, all possible benefit is wiped out
If you hyperventilate, turn blue and pass out.

Aaah!

That's the enthusiastic sound that you might make if someone scratched your back where there was an especially persistent itch. It is also an unwelcome sound that you might make when you are speaking. It seems to happen when people stop to think. It can happen in normal conversations, as well as during formal presentations. People who hear it can ignore that sound once or twice or even a few times but it becomes a distraction if it happens more than that.

Persistent 'aaahs' can damage a speaker's credibility and can destroy the effectiveness of a formal presentation. Saying 'aaah' too often during any verbal communication can affect the way that people perceive your ideas and message. That is really a shame because it is relatively easy to minimize, and maybe even banish, that mannerism from your speech.

This is by far, the greatest single problem that most people have during verbal communications….that is, after they get past the initial fear of speaking before an audience and actually start making public presentations. For some people, it is simply a habit and seems to happen more often when the conversation rambles or when there is a lull in the conversa-

Don Wynn

tion but for most people, it happens when they are thinking about what they are going to say next.

When making a formal presentation, you should know exactly what you plan to say before starting to speak. Practice, practice, practice your presentation beforehand and there will be little need to stop along the way to collect your thoughts. You won't need to stop to think and give the 'aaahs' a chance. Just deliver the presentation you prepared. Pace your presentation and allow yourself to breathe. It is very easy during presentations to speak too fast. Be aware when you breathe not to inadvertently make that noise.

In other business communications, such as conversations with several people, it is best to train yourself to concentrate on listening. If you really listen to the other people in the conversation instead of concentrating on what you will say next you will lessen the tendency to inadvertently make the 'aaah' sound. Additionally, failure to listen to what the other participants are actually saying before you speak usually results in more than just the 'aaah' sound. Actively listening also will help you be more accurate in formulating your responses.

Improvement requires that you make yourself conscious about not making this sound. Once you have done that, you simply need to practice speaking and eliminating the 'aaahs' from your verbal communications.

'Aaah, that's all folks!'

Provide Effective Software and System Demos

As a technology consultant, you may be asked to explain the operation of some aspect of the technology in detail. You may be expected to provide effective software system demonstrations. Your ability to do this with clarity and confidence will have a direct and immediate impact on the way the client perceives you as a consultant and as a representative of your company. Your professional reputation depends how well you can do this!

Most technology consultants have outstanding skills in one or more areas of the technology they work with, and should be able to provide effective software and system demonstrations in those area(s) of expertise.

There is no substitute for preparation. Preparation is paramount, and especially critical if you are currently working in a technological area in which you have limited experience or familiarity. Before the event, ask the client what they expect to see and tailor the demo to meet those specific requirements. Once you have defined the parameters of the demo, you should go through the entire demo in 'practice mode'.

Don Wynn

Exercise every feature and click on every icon that you will discuss in the 'live' demo. You should do this even if you are virtually certain on the outcome. Eliminate the possibility of surprises.

While going through the 'practice' demo, try to anticipate the questions that the client may ask during the 'live' demo. When those questions come up, you will have a ready, confident answer. If those questions do not come up, you can incorporate them to your demo by asking those questions yourself. Avoid asking questions you do not know the answers to. Prepare yourself and become familiar with every nuance of the software beforehand.

You should also incorporate comments into the demo that serve to build confidence the client's confidence in you. For example, you can refer to how certain features of the software were used by past clients. You may not wish identify the client due to confidentiality agreements but you can describe how they used a particular feature. You can also describe a problem that developed at a past client and explain how that problem was solved. One of the greatest benefits you can provide for your clients is to help them avoid problems by providing them the benefit of your experience at multiple sites. If your knowledge is strong but your experience in an area of technology is still 'a work in progress,' ask for help from other consultants who may have more experience in areas relating to the demo you have been requested to present.

Avoid at all costs, clicking on any unfamiliar icon for the

first time in a demo. The result might surprise you! Prepare, familiarize and know the answer before you ask the question or click on an icon.

Unless you are a great juggler, never juggle CD's in front of the client!

Texting Can Be
Dangerous!

Meetings are setup to accomplish specific goals. They are directed activities that deserve the full attention of everyone who attends. Unfortunately, meetings may not always get the level of attention and active participation that they deserve.

The advent of the smart phone is one of the contributors to this problem. These devices can be very handy and useful under the right circumstances but they can also be very destructive under different circumstances. For example, having the ability to access e-mail accounts even when you are away from a traditional computer is very liberating. That capability allows consultants to be fully engaged without being chained to a desk or even to an office.

The ability to send and to receive texts via smart phone is another very good benefit. We can send and receive quick messages that may not require a detailed response. The use of texting in a business environment and business context is becoming more common everyday. Texting is just another technological tool that can be used very effectively under certain circumstances.

Accessing the internet through a browser on a smart phone is another capability that is emerging in importance in the business workplace. More applications are moving to the cloud everyday and the beneficial aspects of internet access by smart phone are growing. The easy access to information on the internet can be a great tool for consultants when used under the right circumstances.

So how does the smart phone impact meetings in a negative way? The answer depends upon how this important tool is being used. Smart phones are a distraction if a meeting participant surfs the web for non-business related information during meetings. For example, going to a streaming news website during meetings is probably not appropriate. Sometimes when a meeting begins to drag, the people in the back of the room may begin to lose interest. Those people could be tempted to surf the web. Professional consultants should resist any temptation to do that.

Texting can also be abused if messages that are unrelated to the meeting are created and exchanged. Consultants should avoid sending texts while in meetings unless those texts are related to the business being discussed. For example, if someone needs to be consulted about a topic that is being discussed, they can be sent a text asking them to come to the meeting. That is a fast and easy way to send an important business message.

If a participant in a meeting is continually checking their smart phone for incoming texts and e-mail, it can be a distraction to the other people in the meeting. If smart phones are continually emitting a tone to indicate activity, that can also be a distraction. If the screen glares, other people around the smart phone user can be distracted. Except in very rare cases, using a smart phone during a meeting is rude, disrespectful of the meeting organizer and the other attendees and is very disruptive.

If you need to use a smart phone during a meeting, the best approach for a consultant to make is to leave the room, use the phone and to return to the room when they are finished using it.

Business Development Is For Business Development People

Well, maybe not! The first step in business development is to identify potential opportunities for business. Who is in a better position to do that than technology consultants themselves?

You are at the front lines in your relationship with your clients. You know intimate details about your client's business and about their business practices. You know their weaknesses and where they are likely to need consulting help in the future. Although, you may not directly make proposals to clients, you can communicate your professional opinions to your consulting company's engagement managers who can make those proposals.

'Out of scope' work also provides some fertile opportunities for you. When someone at a client site asks you to perform 'out of scope' work, you should politely push back because 'scope creep' erodes your company's profitability and takes your attention away from tasks that are 'in scope.' As you politely defer, you should also notify your company's engagement managers to use their negotiating skills to extend your contract, to include tasks that were initially 'out of scope'. Your company's consulting agreements tend to grow over time as clients learn the depth of your individual consulting abilities, as well as and the collective skills of the consulting company you represent. In time, clients come to realize that you and your consulting company can help in areas not covered under the original contract(s).

In addition, you all have a network of professional contacts and should make an effort to use those contacts to develop new business. Every consultant can contribute to their consulting company's business intelligence base by alerting their company's engagement managers regarding possible additional work at their current client site. Don't let your company miss out on an opportunity to submit formal proposals when you are aware of potentially new work fitting your skills, or the skills of other consultants in your company.

Finally, as a consultant, you travel extensively. In most cases, another business traveler is seated next to you on your flights. You can spend a few minutes exchanging pleasantries without becoming that obnoxious row companion who just won't shut up. You should always have business cards available for exchange, who knows, your next big contract could result from a casual conversation you had on an airplane.

My Dad Is Smarter Than Your Dad

Do technology consultants work on the playground? Sometimes it looks like we do. When a discussion about something becomes an argument and all the points have been made, the situation can devolve into something that looks a lot like children squabbling on a playground. The first child says something like, "Because my dad said so." The second child responds, "Well, my Dad said something else and he knows more than your dad." "..Does not." "..Does, too."

The kids keep making statements in a sort of free form flow of random thoughts. Finally, they are wrestling on the ground until they get tired, and then they just start playing again. Adult disagreements usually do not progress to blows or physical wrestling, or at least they shouldn't, and adult verbal combatants may not recover from a disagreement as quickly as kids do. Petty arguments can leave permanent scars on a previously good relationship.

When a consultant gets into this type of exchange, they sometimes fall into a common trap. They cite the number of year's experience that they have or they cite the number of clients that they have served. Those comments are just the technology consulting equivalent of the playground argument.

You should ask yourself two questions. Does it really matter that you have lots of experience? Does it really matter that you have worked at many similar companies with similar challenges? Experience does matter and clients do expect us to have solid experience. They expect that we have worked at a great number of client sites but statistics such as these have little bearing on resolving the issue at hand.

Clients expect us to use our aggregate experience to make convincing arguments about some decision that is to be made. If our experience is as valuable as it should be, we should be able to translate that experience into a compelling discussion without simply citing the statistics of our working lives.

Longevity doesn't mean anything unless you can use that experience to explain a concept or explain your thoughts to the client.

Just Walk Away

Have you ever been angry at work? Unfortunately, for most people, the answer is yes. Have you ever said or done things when you were angry that you regretted later? Unfortunately, the answer to this question is also yes. Anger may be a normal human emotion but outstanding technology consultants find a way to channel their anger so that it does not affect their work in a negative way. It may even be possible to channel your anger to improve the quantity and quality of your work.

Since this situation is so common, it would be a pretty good idea to give some thought to how you should respond when you feel that particular emotion at the client site. The clear objective is that you don't want to do or say anything that you will regret later or that will hurt your relationship with the client.

OK, so what are your options then? You can be aware of your own emotions and concentrate on managing them rather than allowing them to manage you. By thinking about particular scenarios, you will be much better able to handle them when they do come up. You can draw upon a measured response from memory rather than simply react to the cause of your anger as it happens.

One scenario might be in which someone approaches you in

anger or responds to you in an unprofessional way. Your response could diffuse the situation quickly or it could accelerate the situation depending upon what you do. You can respond without compromising your professional integrity or position by saying, "I disagree with your position and would like to explain why." That type of response allows you to keep the conversation focused on the business merits of the argument.

If the other person tries to justify a particular position by citing a 'laundry list' of their accomplishments and work experience, do not respond in kind. You might say, "Even though I have been at many different client sites, I have never seen the situation you mentioned, and even if I had seen that before, I don't think it applies in this case. Let me explain why." Keep the focus on the issue at hand and off of yourself.

If the opposing person says, "When I worked at XYZ Company, that's how we did it." You can say, "We want to apply best practices here and we want to model ourselves after the best companies in our industry. Can you explain more about your idea"? Maintain the focus on the problem, not the people having the problem.

The theme in all of these responses is the explanation. You should be able to explain your position and the other people in the argument should be able to explain theirs. The merits of each position should win the argument.

The volume tends to rise as people get angry. It is important to maintain a reasonable volume to your voice, especially when the other person does not. Some people act as though the loudest voice wins the argument. Do not allow yourself to fall into that trap. In fact, when the situation gets heated, you should concentrate even more on listening so your comments can be a better, more accurate response to what has been said.

If you maintain your composure and professionalism while other people are unable to do the same, you will gain stature in the larger group as a result. The simple act of lowering your voice when the other person raises theirs can bring added credence to your ability to manage the situation.

Finally, if you can tell that you will have difficulty controlling your anger, you need to separate yourself from the source of the anger. If you are in a meeting, you can suggest a postponement and ask, "Can we take a break and resume our meeting in the morning"? Or you can also excuse yourself from the meeting. That may seem awkward but it is certainly better than engaging in a loud public argument at the client site and is far better than losing your temper. Take a walk or go to lunch. Give yourself time to regain control and calm yourself. In the most extreme cases, you may need to leave the client site for the day. Tell someone that you are leaving so as not to just disappear.

Party Hearty

Our work as technology consultants often gives us reason to party, to celebrate some accomplishment as a team. We frequently participate in very large, very stressful projects and completion of these long and complex projects should be celebrated. The team members should take the time to celebrate their individual successes, as well as the successes of the team. It is important to remember as you celebrate with the team to behave in a professional and measured manner.

The team is usually comprised of both consultants and client employees. There will be enough credit for all to share so recognize everyone's contribution, including client employees who provided support that enabled the team to achieve success. Forget any differences that might have transpired along the way because the end result was a team effort. This celebration is part of the 'ego payment' members of the team get at the end of a job well done.

Fun should be an important aspect of the culture at your company. Camaraderie may be part of what drew you to technology consulting, and continues to be a component in the glue that keeps you here.

It is important to remember that your celebrations reflect on your company as a whole. Professional consultants don't throw frat parties. Professional consultants don't embody 'Animal House'. They are professional in every way and always reflect style and grace in their activities. If you work as a technology consultant, you are a professional and you should always have that in mind even when you are celebrating.

Frequently, I have been on consulting teams that were tasked to do a significant amount of cleanup work after previous consultants left a mess. At the end of that initial implementation project those previous consultants likely threw a celebration that does not live up to the standards that a professional should exhibit. My grandmother would say, "They acted a fool!"

Problems with the initial implementation became apparent in the weeks and months following that inappropriate party. The client already had a low opinion of the previous consultants following the party they threw at the conclusion of the project and that low impression was further buttressed by the fact that the previous consultants left the botched project on an artificially high note. When all the problems that were unknown at the conclusion of the initial project were known, the client was left to find another consulting company to clean up the mess the first one had made.

Whether implementing a completely new system or working to resolve the problems caused by the shoddy work of other consultants, you should be especially mindful that the best consultants live up to a high set of professional standards that extend beyond the workday and into those events which follow. Celebration of successes is an important aspect of consulting work but you have to remember to do that with the same style, grace and professionalism with which you approach the balance of your work.

Don Wynn

My Bad!

In the not too distant past, that phrase was apologize for having made a mistake. It responsibility but trivialized the mistake. knowledge responsibility when you have made a mistake and to apologize to the other people who may have been affected by it. It is no secret that it is always better to avoid making a mistake in the first place.

To avoid making mistakes, a consultant must understand the likely contributing factors. The leading factor is the conditions under which consultants work. Consultants work with complex problems and issues, often with severe deadline pressure. Clients expect perfection from technology consultants and consultants should deliver as near to perfection as humanly possible. Now, that's pressure! They expect consultants to be able to answer virtually any question at a moment's notice without referring to any reference material or manual. Whew, just add a little more pressure while you are at it!

Consultants typically feel strongly about their work but must try to separate emotion from their judgments and decision-making. Consultants often work long hours and can have complicated travel schedules, and have responsibilities that extend well beyond their client facing responsibilities. Constant travel, long hours, looming deadlines, fielding complicated questions on the fly, never ending meetings, client requests for demos, throw in a dash of plain old emotion can culminate in..... fatigue. Fatigue can lead to sloppiness which is a precursor to mistakes. See a pattern here?

Given these factors how does a consultant avoid mistakes? The first step is to recognize when a combination of these contributing factors is present then take steps to isolate and control the factors. By taking a few extra minutes to read through a document a second or even third time before transmitting it can dramatically reduce one of the most common areas where mistakes are made. A second pair of eyes reading over your important documents is always a safe bet. But remember to offer the same help to other team members. You can make mistakes on internal documents and communications as easily as you can on deliverables! Everything cannot be reviewed by a peer so reserve that treatment for your more important documents and ideas. This step is in addition to the existing Quality Control step that all deliverable documents should go through. Talk through your ideas with another technology consultant before presenting or acting on them.

We all have deadlines and must manage our time so that you can meet those deadlines. If you have an issue with an approaching deadline you must communicate that concern to your management. You don't know what real pressure is until you spring a nasty last minute surprise on your project manager when earlier notification might have avoided an unfortunate outcome. Never allow deadline pressure to cause mistakes.

Craftsmen never say, "My Bad!" They say, "Measure Twice, Cut Once."

Don Wynn

Avoid Senioritis

Every consulting engagement comes to an end at some point. The client needs consulting support for some period of time, then they resolve the need for that support and the technology consultant is ready for their next job or next assignment. Once the end date is known, some let up in intensity may be normal but the best professional consultants maintain their focus and continue to provide high quality service geared toward the needs of the client.

As some students approach their graduation date, they may tend to lose focus and may develop a case of 'senioritis'. They remember all the work it has taken to get to this particular moment in time and are able to see the end of the race. With their goal in sight they may feel that they can coast across line.

Stopping or easing up before crossing the finish line is a very bad thing to do in technology consulting. Everyone knows value of a good first impression. Not as much attention has been placed on the last or final impression. That last impression can be as important as the first one and can have a lingering effect on a consultant's professional reputation. The first impression may have landed the consultant his current job but it is that final impression that will affect that consultant's ability to land future assignments.

What impression do you leave the client with as you near the end of your assignment? What impression do you want to leave them with? Consultants need a strong set of references. The strongest references are your current and past clients. Their opinion speaks volumes. Hopefully, their trumpet will play a happy tune after you have departed.

Past clients may have a need for your skills and services in the future. It would be a very serious mistake to allow a let-up as you are nearing the end of your current assignment to cause that client to exclude you from consideration for future work. Wouldn't it be a great to score a double entry on your resume by being asked back?

In technology consulting you may need outstanding references to get the best work, your employment opportunities in this field could get slim without them. Former clients who noticed that you were productive on their project right up until your very last day are more inclined to give you a positive recommendation than if you succumb to 'senioritis'.

Like the aging thespian said, "You are only as good as your last performance."

Breaking Bad
......................Habits

Habits are a universal human trait. Everyone does not have the same ones but we all have them. You have acquired your habits throughout your life and may not even know that you have them. Some habits are harmless little things that make us all unique. Other habits can be distracting to your fellow technology consultants and to your clients. When distracting habits exist, it is important to try to reduce any negative impact they might have in your workspace.

Since you may not even be aware of your own habits, what can you do to work on the distracting ones? One thing that you can do is to trust your colleagues. Trust is required when you offer criticism but it is also required when you receive it. Criticism is not pleasant but it is a way to improve. When giving criticism, you should do it respectfully. When receiving criticism, you should do it with grace and with the knowledge that the person offering it is trying to be helpful.

If you see someone exhibit a habit that is distracting to the people around them, you should consider ways to let the person know about the impact they are having. It wouldn't be appropriate to broach the subject in a group. No one would appreciate that. When this type of issue comes up, it should be discussed in a private setting.

Some habits are just annoying but they may not affect your relationships with other consultants or with the client. Other habits are more serious and could dramatically affect you in different ways. Suppose that you have been told that you talk over people in conversations and in meetings. Initially, you may not believe it and may need to prove to yourself that you have that habit. In this case, you could get a small voice-activated recorder. Simply take it to meetings and record the proceedings. That evening, you can replay the recordings you have made. Approach this activity clinically. Try to remove your defensive feelings. Just listen as though you were an impartial observer. Once you have done this, you may be surprised at how prevalent that habit is for you. Your co-worker would never have approached you about it unless they felt that it was more than a minor problem. They believe it is affecting your work and the way that you are perceived in the work place.

If you feel that you don't have that particular habit, you can ask the co-worker who mentioned it to you for some examples. You can enlist their help as coach. They can give you some signal when they believe you are doing it in meetings or in conversations. Maybe they could pull on their ear or something.

Talking over people means that you are not listening. Taking the recorder to meetings will serve as a reminder to you to be conscious of this problem. That little reminder may be enough to help you eliminate or reduce that bad habit but you can do other things as well. Force yourself to mentally count to three after someone finishes speaking before you start speaking. You can ask, "Can I respond now?" which allows the speaker to set the pace of the conversation. The important point is that you do something to address the problem. You may not get any direct feedback but as the problem dissipates, people will begin responding to you in a more positive way. Once a person has been made aware of some negative habit, it should not be a constant topic of conversation between the two people. The person who offered the criticism in the first place is not the judge of the other person. The recipient of the criticism may ask the other person for periodic feedback. If feedback is not requested, the topic should not be discussed again unless the person who has the distracting habit mentions it.

It can be difficult to break habits but it is also important to be aware of the negative ones and to try to reduce them. Try not to become self-conscious of them because that can cause you to highlight them if only subconsciously. You should just make a conscious effort to reduce and to eliminate your bad habits over time. Once you identify a habit that you want to change, how can you accomplish a change? First, you just need to realize that habits are unconscious acts. Changing habits means that you have to bring them up to the conscious level. You need to do something that makes you think of your habits when you are in the situation where they are likely to occur.

For example, if your negative habit is speech related, you can tell someone you trust that you are trying to change that habit. Ask them to remind you when they see your habit. If you show that habit when you are alone with them, they could just remind you. When you are in a group or in front of a room filled with clients, the person could give you a visual cue when they see it. When trying to change negative habits, you may need some good-natured help from your friends and colleagues.

You can also give yourself visual cues that remind you of your negative habit. You can mentally associate your habit with a particular pen or pencil. Whenever you use that pen or pencil, you may remember the habit. You can associate the habit with a single word. Then write the word in the margin of your notebook where you are likely to see it. You can associate the habit with a screen saver so that you see it when you turn your computer on. Women can associate the habit with a particular shade of nail polish or piece of jewelry. You can use your imagination to devise ways to elevate negative habits from the unconscious level to the conscious level where you can alter the habit.

You have to be careful to avoid over concentrating on your negative habit while you are trying to eliminate it. If you become too obsessed with changing your behavior, you can let that effort crowd other thoughts from your conscious mind. If you are making a presentation, concentrate on the material in the presentation but be aware of the negative habit rather than vice versa.

Correcting bad habits takes time and effort on your part but it actually represents an investment you are making in yourself. You will be a better consultant. Your professionalism will increase. You will better represent yourself and your company in the workplace. That sounds like great return on the investment of your time and effort.Breaking bad habits is well worth the effort required.

Don Wynn

So What Do
I Do Now?

Being 'on the bench'
occasionally is a normal
and expected part of the
technology consulting industry.
It results from timing as much as any-
thing else. Resources become available but new projects are
not starting at exactly the same time. The skills of available
resources may not be a good match for the requirements of the
projects that are starting. It becomes a waiting game and even
the best technology consultants sometimes find themselves
waiting for their next assignments.

There are a variety of slang terms used to describe the time
between assignments. Some people describe it as being 'on
the bench' symbolizing a tool that is not in use. Other people
describe it as being 'on the beach' symbolizing a vacation between assignments. Regardless of what this time is called, it
is a period of idle time between assignments.

"So, what do I do now"? That's the question consultants sometimes ask themselves when they complete a project and do not
have another project to go to yet. Hard as it may be to go from
a 'dead run' to a 'full stop' they can simply use the first few
days or even a week to recover from the rigors of the recently
completed project. The 'Go Live' (final project implementation) is typically supported by excessively workdays, including weekends. Bench time can allow people who are tired
from the culmination of their newly completed projects to re-

cover and rejuvenate themselves, and to spend time with their families and friends doing things they couldn't do during the progress of their last project. Rest and relaxation are very important and every person must manage his/her own stamina.

Once a consultant has rested a little and has given him or herself some time to recover, the inevitable question will again be, "So, what do I do now"? A consultant could just sit back and wait for their next assignment but that is not productive and does not further the career goals of the individual or the business goals of their company. One good way to spend this time is for the consultant to consciously do things that will further develop their knowledge and professional skills. Consultants should also do a self-evaluation to determine where they need improvement. In this self-evaluation process, consultants should solicit input from fellow consultants and from company managers. Recent performance appraisals might provide a viable starting point or to think back about things that happened during the consultant's past project(s) which tested the bounds of that consultant's knowledge or skills.

Since technology consulting is so heavily dependent upon emerging technologies and techniques, consultants must continually study these recent innovations to maintain their competitiveness. Consultants can devote their 'bench time' to study and to self-development. These study efforts can be either informal or formal, or a combination of both. Take courses if they are available and pursue additional professional certification when time permits.

Consultants can also use this time to improve their marketability and competitive edge through on-line research and by reading technical reference material. The most important thing for a consultant to remember when they are between assignments is that a successful consulting career requires constant work and study. Time between assignments should be spent as productively as possible.

If You Really Want to Exclude People,
Use Acronyms, Jargon, Buzz Words and Slang

As a profession develops, the language and words used in that profession evolve. Members of the profession begin to use short versions of words that they commonly use. People who are in a profession learn those words pretty quickly through exposure and use and they become a part of the lexicon. They hear these words and begin to use them as a sort of shorthand which increases the pace of conversations. Over time, usage of acronyms, jargon, buzz words and slang become a part of the lexicon and are used almost automatically and without really thinking about it. People don't have to think about them because they know exactly what these words mean. In fact, a person who used an acronym might have to stop and think hard to be able to provide the correct definition for the letters that make it up.

Using these shortcuts is perfectly acceptable as long as everyone really does understand their meanings. The problem is that you can never be really sure that everyone does understand. The possibility of miscommunication increases when a consultant is talking to a group that includes clients or client employees. Those people may not be exposed to other people in the profession very often and may not understand the language. Clients may not want to indicate that they don't know words that everyone else seems to understand easily. It is also possible that the client makes an assumption about the mean-

Don Wynn

ing based upon what they do know. Assumptions are very often wrong and miscommunication is the result.

It is important for technology consultants to be aware of the people they are communicating with. A consultant must sense when someone does not understand the subject of a discussion even when the person does not outwardly indicate anything. That may be difficult to do but the consultant must try.

An alternative would be for the consultant to avoid using short-cut words in conversation unless those words are absolutely necessary to get some point across. Even then, the consultant must be careful. If there appears to be any confusion, the consultant can explain the meaning of the shortcut word that was used or they can steer the conversation in a way that will allow them to determine if the meaning was clear.

When using acronyms or other shortcut words in written communications of any sort, the meaning should be explained the first time the acronym is used. After that, the shortcut can be used in that document without further explanation.

Clear, effective communications are at the core of consulting. The consultant can increase their value to the client if they will limit their use of shortcut words. The best consultants find ways to include the input from more people rather than finding words to exclude people.

Mentoring

Very few people are able to develop consultant level skills without the active help and mentoring from other people in their lives and especially from other, more seasoned consultants. Someone offered a little extra help when some problem arose. They took extra time and answered every question. They anticipated questions and they answered questions that should have been asked but weren't. They served as a special type of friend in a professional context.

Mentor is not a title that can be given to a person by a company. It doesn't fit on an organizational chart and doesn't belong on a business card. Mentor is a title that only the recipient can bestow. It represents an acknowledgement of the impact that the mentor is having on the life of the person who awarded the title. To be called a mentor is a great honor and this title should be treated with reverence and respect.

Usually a mentor is older than the student but that isn't necessarily the case. The most important traits for a mentor to have are knowledge, experience and a willingness to share the lessons they have learned with someone else. People will usually respond well to shared knowledge as long as that knowledge is shared the right way.

Mentoring can happen in groups where a single person explains a given topic and answers questions from a group. That model sounds more like a formal class than it sounds like a mentoring session. Some mentoring sessions may be scheduled but the most effective and rewarding sessions seem to happen on an impromptu basis. They usually occur in one to one sessions rather than in larger groups. Since mentoring has an impromptu nature and since mentoring sessions address some issue immediately as it comes up, it is almost impossible to schedule mentoring classes.

It may be possible for a company to teach their more senior consultants some of the methods that effective mentors use but knowledge of mentoring skills alone does not make someone a mentor. Earning that title from a student depends upon how the prospective mentor applies their new knowledge of mentoring skills. In my view, it is a professional responsibility to seek mentoring opportunities and to provide helpful information to people who are just entering the profession.

One very negative reaction that prospective students can have when they first become consultants is their failure to recognize the fact that they could use help. The perception seems to be that consultants are supposed to know everything. That is ridiculous and is impossible but new consultants seem reluctant to acknowledge that they don't know something as though their acknowledgement would mean that they are not consultants after all.

Prospective students should accept help when it is offered and they should realize that the person offering it is doing them a great service. At some point, the student will become the master and will serve as a mentor to a new generation.

Professional Bearing

Some people just seem to be ideally suited to their professions. People around them recognize their suitability and give them added credibility as a result. Have you ever known someone like that? What gave you the impression that they are someone you might learn something from?

Initial impressions are usually formed before you learn much about their actual knowledge, skills or experience. If you are not familiar with their technical skills, what about them caught your attention? Perhaps, it is what we might refer to as professional bearing. The person just looks and acts like a professional.

These people exhibit certain intangible qualities; characteristics you cannot see, feel or touch but you recognize them anyway. Ever notice how people who stand erect and sit up straight appear taller and more alert. Well, that simple conscious act can convey a message of confidence, and that that person is aware of his/her surroundings. Is it possible to develop such a 'presence' without appearing arrogant? Most of us would like to develop that special personal demeanor that seems to silently lend an air of credibility and professionalism to that person, even before they ever open their mouth. Now

Don Wynn

you ask, "Where can I buy some, how much does it cost, and does it come in travel size"?

First, you might study that person's actions, mannerisms, physical bearing, attire, tenor of their voice, etc. to determine which you might be able to adopt or closely emulate? You are not attempting to be that person's 'mini me' but you can learn from that person's style. Incorporate those characteristics and intangibles which you think fit your personal style.

You can never go wrong with a good personal appearance. This is not an intangible so incorporating this in you regimen is a no-brainer that everyone can benefit from and others will appreciate. Attention to personal grooming may just top the list in its importance. Keep your hair trimmed and neat, the particular style is not important but it must appear that you take personal grooming seriously.

Beards are fine but they project a much stronger impression if they are well tended. That day-old-stubble look may be popular in your personal activities but you should make sure it gives the impression you want to convey before introducing that look at the client site.

Colognes or perfumes can be tricky, use them sparingly, if at all. Don't let your 'essence' precede you into a room and linger after you are gone. And no one likes to pick up an office telephone and come away smelling like the person who used it previously.

Emphasis should also be placed on your attire next. Basic rules apply; you should not go to your workplace looking shabby, rumpled, stained or generally unkempt. Going to work sporting the look of an 'unmade bed' will not convey anything positive about you. Careless grooming makes you look careless and as if you don't hold yourself to any particular personal standard. You may not be careless in your work but your appearance can suggest that you are.

Shoes do more than just cover your feet; they quietly announce that you pay attention to the details.....a very positive sign when your particular profession requires precision and attention to detail. Shoes should be clean, in good repair and have a recent coat of polish. You may still work in your weathered and worn footwear, that is, work you do in your personal time in your yard or home garage.

Grubby or jagged fingernails might not be particularly important to your profession but what if your physician came into the examination room like that? You would notice. Your colleagues may take note of which keyboard you use. As your clothes, shoes and ties begin to show evidence of wear or become stained, retire those articles from your professional wardrobe.

You may be asking, what has all of this to do with the quality of your work. Well, the simple answer is, probably not much. You can still be a great consultant if you are messy or rumpled but if you wish to be afforded added stature and credibility in your profession you might pay attention to your personal details first. You are your own personal billboard.

This brings to mind a brokerage firm advertisement of yesteryear that stated, "When E.F. Hutton speaks, every one listens." This means you are going to have to do more than 'talk the talk' (the proverbial empty-suit), you will have to 'walk the walk'.

Your Resume

There is an entire industry dedicated to the preparation of effective resumes so I won't go into much detail here. I simply want you to realize that the resume is one of your most valuable 'tools' in your toolbox. Next in line of importance is your cover letter. Take special care in creating these documents as they will serve as your 'personal ambassador' and will determine whether or not you get an interview. They can open doors for you if well presented. Create your 'personal ambassador' with a few basic, yet important, elements in mind.

Your resume must be complete yet concise, businesslike yet personable. The overall appearance of your resume must be neat and organized; events must be logically sequenced while reflecting a balanced appearance. The reader formulates his/her initial impression of you within minutes after picking up your resume. You will have made a serious mistake if the content of your resume must overcome a bad first impression.

The first page must be aesthetically pleasing, inviting the reader to meet you in person. The entire document must be easy to read. Use of bolding or italicized words should be reserved for the things that are really important. If you use those features too much, they will not have the desired effect and may even detract from your overall message.

Font and font size are important, too. It may be tempting to use some obscure font or one that has flourishes. Scroll looks pretty but can be hard to read. In my experience, it is better to use a standard font that you would encounter on regular business correspondence. Times New Roman is the font used by many different newspapers because it is easy to read. Regardless of the font that you use, the reviewer should not even notice the font and will concentrate on the text of the resume. If you choose to use an obscure font thinking its style difference will set your resume apart from the rest, the reader will notice and could become distracted from the actual content of your resume. Your message should be read, not deciphered.

Vary font size for headings and for basic content but don't use too many different ones. Do not use more than three sizes. If in doubt, two might be better. Your contact information should be in the largest font in your resume….but don't 'YELL." Headings can be in a second font size and basic content can be in a slightly smaller font size. Use of colored paper and different color ink, like red or blue, take more effort to read and you don't want this to be the reason your resume was placed at the bottom of the reader's pile.

Once the reader actually starts reading your resume, the most important aspect comes into play. Truthfulness is the most important element in the text of your resume. Stories abound regarding 'pretenders' who list accomplishments, education, awards and experience in their resumes that are pure fabrication. That is a huge mistake and will ultimately cause issues for you if you do it. The reader may even become suspicious if you claim to have received more training or more experience than is reasonable for the stated period of time.

Those falsified credentials may get past the reader and you into an interview. You may even get the job but the client will right-fully expect you to perform based upon your falsifications. If your deception is not found out immediately, it eventually will be. The result will be extremely bad.

Present your education, experience, special qualifications and accomplishments as positively as you can but do not fabri-cate. There are some things that can be left to interpretation but other things are simply, 'yes or no'. You either earned that specific degree or honor or you did not. If you are ap-plying for an assignment that needs specific experience and skills, it is perfectly reasonable to highlight your experience and skill in that particular area but expect closer questioning and scrutiny in a later phase of your job search. If you earned certain experience, and the job description fits your experience or background then craft your resume and cover letter with that assignment in mind. That is acceptable and will help the reviewer decide if you are a strong enough candidate to invest an interview in you.

Buzz-words and acronyms can be important on your resume because some companies use computer searches designed to locate only resumes containing specific words or phrases. Make use of these keywords but avoid overusing them. The computer may hone in on those words but once that resume gets into the reader's hands it could come across like Morse code. There is no formula that can tell you what the right amount so you have to depend upon your instincts and judgment.

The objective of your resume and cover letter are to get you past the initial resume review phase and into the interview process. Present your skills and experience in such a way that the reviewer will want to discuss your qualifications with you. A well-written resume simply opens that door and introduces you, just like a 'personal ambassador' would.

If you aren't getting called for interviews, the fault could lie in the way you present yourself in your resume. Review your current resume, consult others who have used resumes successfully and try to incorporate some of the simple tips outlined above. It might be a good idea to get a second opinion from an unbiased reader (not your mother or spouse, they are never unbiased).

The Interview

Your resume served as your advance team or 'personal ambassador' and opened the door to the interview. It demonstrated your ability to convey in writing important information about yourself and highlighted your qualifications for a particular job. It did its job and got you the opening interview. The next step gets trickier.

The interview process is usually made up of a series of interviews rather than just one. In the interview phase your interpersonal skills and verbal abilities will take center stage. Rejection can come at any step in this process. After each interview, you should be pleased if you are invited to another interview.

The first interview will likely be to determine if you are a good fit for the company. The interviewer may not be quite as knowledgeable about what you do as succeeding interviewers will be. This interview will be evaluating your appearance, attire, demeanor and verbal abilities. The interviewer will also be assessing your body language, eye contact and other outward signs of poise and confidence.

During this initial interview you may be encouraged to ask questions. The questions you ask will be evaluated by the interviewer, as will everything else you do and say during the interview. Do not lose sight of the fact that the interviewer is more interested in the benefit you can provide to them rather than in the benefit they can provide to you. Your questions should be crafted to show that you have interest in that specific assignment and that you understand the nuances of the work. Your having done a little research about the company you are applying to prior to the interview could win you valuable points with the interviewer, too.

Be cautioned, this is the wrong time to ask about compensation, benefits or about policies related to expense statements. As you move through the interview process, there will be a time for that type of question but that time is near the end of the process, and should occur only after it is clear that you are the candidate that will be hired. That time is definitely not during the first interview.....unless, of course, you are so wonderful that they hire you on the spot.

The interviewer will also be evaluating statements that you make. Statements made in the interview could have a more serious impact than you could ever guess. For example, you may want to let the interviewer know that you will be a good fit for the position. How you convey this enthusiasm is important. You might be tempted to say, "I think I am perfect for the position and I believe I am going to enjoy working here." That statement implies that you have already been hired and may send a negative message to the interviewer.

Perhaps a more subtle and sophisticated approach would be to say, "I believe I would be a good fit for the position based upon what you have told me, and I would welcome the opportunity to work here." That statement will have a much more positive impact.

Succeeding interviews will become increasingly more focused on your skills and less on your 'fitness' within the company culture. That does not mean that interpersonal skills, appearance and demeanor are any less important just because the emphasis of this interview has shifted to your direct job-related skills.

After you have worked as a consultant for some period of time, you will most likely have more experience in the interview process than the interviewer will have. Age and experience do have their advantages! Use that experience to your advantage. The interviewer may likely ask the same set of questions of every person being interviewed. If the interviewer asks questions that have 'yes or no' answers, you should elaborate on your answer so the interviewer learns something tangible about you.

If others being interviewed provide only 'yes' or 'no' answers, your answers will make you stand out in a positive way. The interviewer will most likely remember you because you provided qualification with your answers. Guard against providing more information than the question calls for because even interviewers have schedules to keep....and their attention span may not allow for the influx of too much information. In short, make your answers concise tailoring your responses to address the point of each question. Such elaboration can improve your chances of getting another interview, and of potentially getting the assignment.

Don Wynn

The Best Offer

Prospecting for clients and for your next consulting assignment is a normal and expected part of work as a consultant. Success depends upon the continued development of a network of contacts in the field while maintaining an awareness of potential opportunities for future work. This applies to both the independent contractor and to consultants employed by a consulting company.

Successful consultants endeavor to develop their professional reputations, as well as their network of contacts. These consultants can expect to receive frequent inquiries about their availability for new assignments. Telephone calls and e-mails inquiring as to a consultant's availability should be welcomed but they should never provide an inducement to abandon a current client before the current assignment has concluded. Realizing that consultants sometimes may need to leave an assignment before it is completed but that should be a rare occurrence and should never for financial gain. 'Jumping ship' may bring immediate financial gain but this industry has a long memory and will result in future negative consequences when it is perceived that a consultant cannot be relied upon to fulfill his/her obligations.

When a consultant reaches an agreement with a client to join a project, the consultant should feel an obligation to remain on the project until culmination. In some cases, consultants are contract bound for a specified period of time but the obligation referenced here is not the legal obligation imposed by that type of contract. The consultant has a professional obligation to support the client and to provide the highest possible level of service throughout the project even if a legal obligation to do that does not exist.

Since income and other financial arrangements can change from project to project, it can be very tempting to accept the highest offer regardless of the impact that a decision to leave can have on the existing client. When a consultant does that, they are making long term sacrifices for short term gains. Leaving a client before the end of a project can have a lasting impact on career development and a history of doing that can reduce the consulting opportunities that are offered to you in the future.

When an inquiry is received from a prospective client or from a recruiter, it is not necessary to refuse to discuss the future with them. However, it is necessary to honestly discuss your availability. For example, you could say, "I am obligated on a project for the next three months. I expect to be available at that time. Will that meet the requirements of your schedule"? When you start the conversation like that, you have been honest with the prospective client and have expressed a commitment to your existing client. You have expressed your professionalism and the prospective client will understand and appreciate that.....and will most likely call back later because you will have indicated that you are loyal and trustworthy..... and are as good as your word.

Recognizing Client Employee Fears

One aspect of a consultant's work is to help clients and their employees understand, accept and work through the changes that new technology systems will bring. Resistance by client employees is one of the most significant threats to the success of any technology project. The most successful projects require client employees to understand the necessity for changes and to work together with the consultant(s).

In order to foster the acceptance of change, consultants should understand the source of employee resistance. Fear is the root cause of resistance by employees, and it is in the consultant's, and the best interest of the consultant's company, to work to alleviate fear as it as much as possible. Client employee fear can be classified into 4 distinct categories:

Can I keep up? Employees can sometimes be fearful of their ability to learn the new technology with its attendant policies, procedures and methods. They often ask themselves, "Can I keep up; can I learn this"? Age could play a part in that fear but anyone can suffer from it regardless of their age.

Will I lose my status? Employees can sometimes be fearful that they will lose their status as experts in the old policies, procedures and methods. Some employees may be recognized as the 'go to' people by their peers. That status could be lost as a result of the project you are working on. These employees fear that having to learn a new system will put them on the same playing field as every other employee. The potential loss of status is a very real fear for people who have mastered the old system.

Will I lose my job? Potential for job loss is a strong fear for employees because many technology projects are justified by the anticipated employee reductions that could result. Employees have seen other projects at their company and at other companies where jobs were eliminated as soon as the new project started producing results. On the other hand, the failure of an employee to learn the new technology may possibly result in the loss of a job.

We have nothing to fear but fear itself. Some employees may have vague fears of the unknown, while others simply distrust management and anything management does. The hardest employee for the consultant to convince that new technology will be of benefit is the generally untrusting personality, because for this employee the project represents change, change equals uncertainly, and disruption of any kind is unwelcome.

The message here is that a successful consultant will endeavor to recognize and be aware of the forces behind resistance, and that the antidote requires education and plenty of patience.

Don Wynn

Recognize the Fears of Project Managers

Project Manager is a unique position at most client sites and represents a tremendous career opportunity for the people who are chosen for those positions. The project manager is often perceived by the client company as the most talented and capable employee at the client site. The project manager understands technology and the benefits that the company can achieve by embracing it. They have organizational and managerial skills that have earned them the respect of management and employees alike.

The position of project manager provides an opportunity to further demonstrate those capabilities. The project manager can differentiate him/herself from other employees while preparing themselves for even more responsibility. Their careers will be affected by the direction and outcome of the projects they lead.

Even though, they may never express it, fear is a normal part of the life of most project managers. They fear project failure. They fear the unknown. They fear the actions of members of their teams.

Project managers usually are type-A personalities who are accustomed to being in charge and in control. However, their performance, and that of the project, is often under far closer scrutiny by company managers than they might be accustomed to, and they might have less managerial latitude than they are used to having. Project managers usually lead large diverse teams of employees recruited from throughout the client organization. Not every team member is as dedicated or as responsible as the project manager. In addition, the project manager must coordinate the employees under his/her direction with outside consultants.

It is easy to recognize that project managers typically experience a lot of tension and stress associated with their jobs because with them rests the responsibility for everything that happens on the project. The career of the project manager may be at stake. Project success will most definitely lead to career advancement; project failure will almost certainly damage career prospects. The project manager may survive a failed project but it could easily take years to recover. To fully recover, the project manager may feel compelled to change companies to get a new start.

Under these circumstances, a project manager can be expected to act even more driven and task oriented than they normally would. A consultant should recognize the stress that the project manager is under and do things to maintain focus on the most serious threats to project success. When a situation or issue arises, the consultant should take the time to formulate possible solutions and avoid simply reporting the problem.

At the end of the project, there will be an assessment of the success of the project, and the project manager wants his/her performance to be viewed in a positive light, despite the outcome of the project. The consultant will probably be leaving the client company to go to their next project but, in almost every case, the consultant leaves with more blame for things that did not go as well as expected than they deserve.

Exit Strategies

When you work as a consultant, you frequently transition from one client site to the next. That transition period offers opportunities for the consultant that should not be overlooked. Leaving the client with a good impression of you and of your professionalism increases the likelihood of receiving a positive recommendation in the future. This period may also offer an opportunity to ask that client to serve as a reference for future work. Such benefits can accrue if you are mindful of how important these finals days can be.

Never leave an assignment unfinished. Complete your assigned tasks and ensure the client understands what you have accomplished. If some issue prevents you from completing an assigned task, make sure to discuss the current status of that task with the client. Provide the reason(s) you were unable to finish that task or assignment. Formally documenting the status of all unfinished or unaddressed assignments is of paramount importance. This document will be your representative should questions arise later as to what was, or was not done, and why; it also will document the fact that you discussed this with the client prior to your departure. Future assignments depend heavily upon how past clients view you and your company.

It is usually good business etiquette to provide the client with contact information where you can be reached if they need to discuss any aspect of your work. Give the client a business card with your contact information on it along with a follow-up e-mail. Provide information as to your availability if there are restrictions on your time at your next client site. For example, you can say, "You can reach me at this number and at this e-mail address during normal business hours. Please call me if you ever need my input about anything. If I don't answer immediately, I should respond within a few hours."   Since past clients very seldom call, I usually tell them that I will take their calls anytime without restriction.

In the days leading up to your final day at the client site, you should return anything that was provided to you by the client. Some clients may provide a laptop or security medallions to use while working on their project. Turn in these items along with any security badges or cards that provided you with access to client facilities. Return all client property and request a receipt.

If you have worked on a desktop or laptop computer at the client site, you should save any files that must be retained by the client.   Provide the client with a copy of the pertinent files. These files can be stored on a network drive, emailed or be placed on some portable storage medium that you give to the client. Once those files have been provided to the client, you should delete any work files or cache that remains on the systems you used. This is just a good business practice and prevents unnecessary files from clogging their equipment.

Leave your physical work area uncluttered. Remove old files and clutter from your entire work area including desk drawers and file cabinets.   If you have clipped anything to in-office boards, remove those items. When you leave your area, it should be ready for the next person to immediately move into the space.

A personal acknowledgement of the people you worked with while at the client site is very important too. You can accomplish this important step in several ways. Send an e-mail expressing gratitude for having had the opportunity to work with them on the project and briefly highlight some of the accomplishments that the team achieved. You should include your contact information and request theirs. Try to visit briefly with each person if possible; face to face meetings are perfect just as you are exiting the client facilities for the last time. Keep the departure visits short and exiting with a good, firm handshake along with a sincere message will help the client remember you.

Saying "good-bye" is never easy to do but if you do it right, you will leave the client with a very positive impression of you.

Coming Release from Don Wynn

The Handbook of Technology Consulting
available 2013

This book will provide more information that every
consultant should know. It will explain things about the
consulting profession that will save new consultants time
and effort.

This book will benefit people who aspire to become
consultants as well as people who are already working as
consultants.

This book will not cover the topics that are being consulted upon.

Partial List of Topics Covered

- Realities in the technology consulting marketplace.
- Consulting Business Models
- What is required
- What do consultants do and not do
- Making the transition into consulting
- What do consultants and clients owe each other
- Financial Considerations
- Burdens on personal life
- Payment and billing methods
- Assignment types
- Work Methods
- Travel Considerations
- Work Conditions
- Work Schedules
- Soft Skills
- Finding Work
- International Assignments
- Before you arrive at the client site
- Last week/day at the client site

Availbility as a Speaker
at Meetings and Conferences

Don is available as a speaker for meetings and conferences. His presentations are both entertaining and informative and would be appropriate for almost any group. His story telling style makes his presentations unforgettable.

Attendees will come away from the presentation with smiles on their faces but they will also have specific knowledge that they will be able to apply in their daily activities.

For information, please e-mail don.wynn@ thebrasstree.com. Include 'Speaking Engagement' in topic line of your e-mail.